Innovating
University Education
Issues in Contemporary African Higher Education

A Book in Honour of Makerere University's
90 Years of Excellence 1922–2012

Editors

Jude Ssempebwa
Peter Neema-Abooki
J.C.S. Musaazi

FOUNTAIN PUBLISHERS
www.fountainpublishers.co.ug

Fountain Publishers
P. O. Box 488
Kampala
E-mail: sales@fountainpublishers.co.ug
publishing@fountainpublishers.co.ug
Website: www.fountainpublishers.co.ug

On behalf of
East African School of Higher Education Studies and Development, College of Education and External Studies, Makerere University

Distributed in Europe, North America and Australia by African Books Collective Ltd (ABC), Unit 13, Kings Meadow, Ferry Hinksey Road, Oxford OX2 0DP, United Kingdom.
Tel: 44(0) 1865–726686, Fax: 44(0)1865–793298.
E-mail: abc@africanbookscollective.com
Website: www.africanbookscollective.com

© The authors 2017
First published 2017

All rights reserved. No part of this publication may be reprinted or reproduced or utilised in any form or by any means, electronic, mechanical or other means now known or hereafter invented, including copying and recording, or in any information storage or retrieval system, without permission in writing from the publishers.

ISBN 978-9970-25-935-9 (paper back)

ISBN 978-9970-25-945-8 (ebook)

Cover design: Ritah N. Edopu. Photos (Clockwise): 1. Makerere University Main Building (Side view from the South-East) in 1941; 2. Some staff and students of Makerere College in 1938; 3. L-R: Presidents Julius K. Nyerere (Tanzania), Jomo Kenyatta (Kenya) and Kenneth Kaunda (Zambia) in procession at the inauguration of Makerere University on 8th October 1970; 4. President Yoweri K. Museveni takes a joy ride in Kiira EV (a vehicle design project of Makerere University's College of Engineering, Design, Art and Technology) to mark its official launch on 24th November 2011; 5. HRH Edward A.C.G.A.P. David, Prince of Wales (later King Edward VIII), and Makerere College Principal Mr Douglas G. Tomblings inspecting the College in 1928.

Dedication

To the memory of Sir Philip Euen Mitchell
(Governor of Uganda, 1935–1940)

Contents

Dedication .... *iii*
Contributors .... *ix*
Tables .... *xix*
Acronyms .... *xxi*
Foreword .... *xxiii*
Preface and Acknowledgements .... *xxvii*

Chapter: 1   **Higher Education for Innovation and Development** 1
Haruna Yakubu
Introduction 1
Higher Education and National Science, Technology and
Innovation Capacity 3
What is the Purpose of Higher Education? 8
Foundation for Capacity Building 11
Communication of Science and Technology Innovation ... 12
Conclusion 17

Chapter: 2   **Challenges and Opportunities for Quality Assurance of
Cross-Border Higher Education in East Africa** 18
Philipo Lonati Sanga
Introduction 18
Rationale for Cross-Border Higher Education 20
Benefits of and Threats to Cross-Border Higher Education ... 21
Quality Assurance for Higher Education in East Africa 22
Challenges in Implementing Cross-Border Higher Education
in East Africa 25
Opportunities of Implementing Cross-Border Higher
Education in East Africa 30
Conclusion 32

Chapter: 3 William Senteza-Kajubi as a Change Agent in Uganda's Education System with Specific Reference to Widening Access to University Education 34
Fred E. K. Bakkabulindi
Introduction 34
Who was Senteza-Kajubi? 36
Purpose 38
Method 38
Widening Access to University Education for Primary School Teachers 39
Widening Access to University Education for Secondary School Teachers 41
Calling for the Massification of Access to Public Universities 42
Calling for the Opening of Private Universities 44
Grooming Nkumba University to Maturity 45
Discussion and Recommendations 49

Chapter: 4 Deregulation of Higher Education in Nigeria: A Call for Restraint 51
A. O. K. Noah, Adesoji A. Oni & Stephen D. Bolaji
Introduction 51
Deregulation in Nigeria 52
Deregulation of University Education in Nigeria 53
Problems Associated with Deregulation of Higher Education 54
Conclusion and Way Forward 57

Chapter: 5 Do Universities in Uganda Satisfy their International Students? 58
Jude Ssempebwa, Fawz N. Mulumba & Ritah N. Edopu
Introduction 58
Methodology 62
Findings 65
Discussion and Recommendations 67

Chapter: 6 Attributes of Human Capital Developed by Ugandan Universities and Students' Post-Graduation Motives 70
Livingstone Ddungu
Introduction 70
Related Literature and Knowledge Gap 71
Methodology 77
Findings and Discussion 78

Chapter: 7	The Importance of Research in a University 85
	Mahmood Mamdani
	Introduction 85
	History of Higher Education in Africa 86
	A Pervasive Consultancy Culture.................................... 88
	Reflections on Postgraduate Education in the Humanities and the Social Sciences 92
	The Postgraduate Initiative at MISR............................... 94
Chapter: 8	University Governance and Intellectual Capital at two Universities in Uganda 99
	Karim N. A. Ssesanga
	Introduction 99
	Related Literature.. 101
	Methodology... 103
	Findings and Discussion 104
	Conclusions and Recommendations.............................. 116
Chapter: 9	Prospective Graduates' Perception of the Responsiveness of Ethiopian Universities to Contemporary Labour Market Needs 117
	Demewoz Admasu Gebru
	Introduction 117
	Methodology... 121
	Findings and Interpretation... 122
Chapter: 10	Challenges of University Governance in Malawi 127
	Lester Brian Shawa
	Introduction 127
	Global Policy-Steerage and University Governance 128
	New Managerialism and University Governance in Malawi...... 130
	The Interventionist Nature of University Governance in Malawi 135
	Conclusion 138
Chapter: 11	Organisational Commitment of Academic Staff at Universities in Uganda 139
	Edith Namutebi & John Baptist Mpoza
	Introduction 139
	Research Framework 144
	Findings and Discussion 147

Chapter: 12 Viability of Open Educational Resources in Open and Distance Learning: Views of Members of the Executive Board of the African Council for Distance Education, Kenya 153
Vincent Ado Tenebe & Rotimi Ogidan
Introduction 153
Concept and Potential of OERs 154
Questions and Approach 156
Viability of OERs in ODL in Africa 159

Chapter: 13 Stereotype Threat and University of Botswana Teacher Trainees' Attitude towards their Training Programme and Teaching .. 161
H. Johnson Nenty, Phuti Fiji & Moyo Sello
Introduction 161
Background 162
Related Literature 166
Methodology and Findings 169
Discussion 173
Conclusion 175
References 176
Index 205

Contributors

A.B.K. Kasozi (PhD) is a research associate at Makerere Institute of Social Research (MISR). He is the founding Executive Director of Uganda's National Council for Higher Education (NCHE). He holds a B.A. in History, a PGD from Makerere University, Uganda, and a PhD from the University of California at Santa Cruz. He has taught at Makerere University, the Islamic University in Uganda, the University of Khartoum and a number of universities in Canada. In 2007, he got a Fulbright New Century award and was, from September to December, a visiting scholar/professor at Teachers College, Columbia University, New York. He is the author of University Education in Uganda: Opportunities and Challenges for Reform of Higher Education (Fountain Publishers, Kampala, 2003); The Social Origins of Violence in Uganda, 1964-85 (Montreal/Kingston: McGill-Queens University Press, 1994), The Crisis of Secondary School Education in Uganda, 1960-70, (Longman, 1979); The Spread of Islam in Uganda (Oxford University Press, 1979), The Life of Prince Badru Kakungulu (Progressive Publishers, 1996), Islamic Civilization in Eastern Africa (Ed.) (Istanbul: IRCICA, 2008): Financing Uganda's public universities (Fountain Publishers, Kampala, 2009) and several articles.

    Adesoji A. Oni (PhD) is a senior lecturer in the Department of Educational Foundations, Faculty of Education, University of Lagos, Nigeria. He specialises in Sociology of Education and Foundation Studies in Education. His area of research focus includes social problems in education, teacher education, social change in education and social deviances in education—with particular focus on cultism in Nigerian HEIs. He has published widely in these areas, with over 100 publications to his credit. In 2003, he won the Fulbright Visiting Scholar Fellowship to Southern Illinois University. Oni is also the Secretary and Managing Editor of Journal of Educational Review of the Higher Education Research and Policy Network (HERPNET).

Anyikwa Blessing Egbichi (PhD) is a lecturer in the Department of Adult Education, Faculty of Education, University of Lagos, Nigeria. She holds a BEd (Adult Education) of the University of Ibadan and a Master's and PhD from the University of Lagos. She is the coordinator of the Literacy Centre of the University of Lagos. She is a member of the Teachers Registration Council of Nigeria (TRCN) and the Nigerian National Council for Adult Education (NNACE). She specialises in literacy, adult psychology and teaching methods.

Demewoz Admasu Gebru (PhD) is assistant professor of higher education policy, governance and leadership at the Department of Education, College of Teacher Education, Kotebe University College (Addis Ababa) where he is also the Vice-President for Academic and Research Affairs.

Edith Namutebi (PhD) is a lecturer in the Faculty of Education, Mutesa I Royal University, where she is also in charge of research and pre-service school practice. A holder of a BA with Education, MSc. in Human Resource Management in Education and PhD in Educational Management from Makerere University, Doctor Namutebi is an experienced educator who has served at various levels of Uganda's education system. Her current research focuses on the management of human resources in universities in Uganda.

Fawz N. Mulumba (PhD) is a former Director of the Directorate of Quality Assurance at Kampala International University (KIU) and is the founding director of the International Network for Education in East Africa (INEEA). A holder of a BA, Ed and MEd (Econ.) from Makerere University and a PhD (Ed Mgt) from KIU, Fawz is a founding member of the Uganda Universities Quality Assurance Forum (UUQAF). He is also a visiting lecturer at the Islamic University in Uganda (IUIU) and KIU (Dar es Salaam). His research focuses on cross-border modes of higher education delivery, international student flows and quality assurance in international higher education.

Fiji Phuti is a tutor in the area of research and evaluation at Botswana College of Distance and Open Learning. She holds a BEd (Home Economics) and a Master of Education (Research and Evaluation). Presently, she is pursuing doctoral studies in the area of research and evaluation. She is a member of the Botswana Education Research Association and a former President of the University of Botswana Home Economics Society. Phuti has spoken at national and international conferences and published in a range of international journals.

Fred E.K. Bakkabulindi (PhD) is an associate professor of educational research, statistics and evaluation at the East African School of Higher Education Studies and Development (EASHESD), College of Education and External Studies (CEES), Makerere University. He is also a member of the University's Senate. A holder of a Bachelors of Statistics and a Postgraduate Diploma in Computer Science of Makerere University; a Master of Science of Southampton University, UK; and a PhD of Makerere University, he has taught research, statistics and related subjects since 1988 at Makerere University, Uganda Management Institute, Makerere University Business School, Uganda Martyrs

University, Nkumba University, Kisubi Brothers University College and Kampala International University. He is a member of the Uganda Statistical Society (USS) and Higher Education Research and Policy Network (HERPNET). His current research interests focus on the adoption of innovations in higher education institutions (HEIs) and on doctoral pedagogies.

H. Johnson Nenty is a professor of educational research, measurement and evaluation in the Department of Educational Foundations, University of Botswana. He is a devotee of item response theory (IRT), which he is acclaimed to father in Africa. With 35 years of experience in the area, he spreads the 'gospel' of educational measurement according to IRT by publishing, teaching, and supervising doctoral students and offering consultancy services in the area. In addition to similar previous appointments, he has just been appointed the editor-in-chief of African Journal of Theory and Practice of Educational Assessment and African Journal of Theory and Practice of Educational Research of the Educational Assessment and Research Network in Africa (EARNiA).

Haruna Yakubu (PhD) is the Vice-Chancellor of the University for Development Studies, Ghana. Formerly, he was Pro-Vice Chancellor of the University of Cape Coast; Chairman of the Governing Council of the Centre for Renewable Energy Studies (CRES); member of Ghana Solar Energy Society; fellow of Education-UK; associate member of the International Centre for Theoretical Physics (ICTP); and member of the governing council of the Foundation for Security and Development in Africa (FOSOA).

J. C. S. Musaazi (PhD) is the founding Principal of the CEES where he is also a professor of Education. He has over 25 years' experience in government, international and private organisations. He is an expert in the fields of Higher Education, Education Management, Human Resource Management, Financial Management, Educational Planning, Development Administration, Research Methods, Strategic Planning and Development Education. He has carried out consultancy and research projects with the National Council of Education in Jamaica, the World Bank, USAID, Caribbean Community Secretariat, Inter-American Development Bank, UNESCO, UNDP and DFID. He has held a number of Commonwealth Chairs, including Rector of Lesotho College of Education and Director of Education Research, University of the West Indies, Kingston, Jamaica. He also served as the head of the Department of Higher Education, now the EASHESD, Makerere University. He was also appointed director of the Education Policy Centre, University of Fort Hare, South Africa. For several years, he was Head of Educational Planning, Administration and Management at Ahmadu Bello University, Zaria, Nigeria, where he also acted as Dean, Faculty of Education. He was also appointed a senior research professor at the University of the Western Cape, South Africa. Professor Musaazi was also a Senior Consultant and Trainer in Behavioural and Management Sciences for the East African Community and was Head of the Training and Consultancy Department. He also acted as Principal Secretary, Directorate of Personnel Management, Office of the President, Nairobi, Kenya. In addition, he has authored several books in the area of education management and contributed many articles to a variety of learned journals.

John Baptist Mpoza (PhD) is a lecturer of education management at Kisubi Brothers University Constituent College of Uganda Martyrs University and a member of the governing council of Mutesa I Royal University. A holder of a PhD (Education Planning and Administration) from, Makerere University, he is an experienced educationist with over 30 years of teaching and administering at various levels of the education system.

Joshua Rotimi Ogidan (PhD) is a professor of Guidance and Counselling in the School of Education, National Open University of Nigeria (NOUN). He studied Guidance and Counselling in the University of Ilorin for his BEd, MEd and PhD programmes in 1987, 1989 and 1999, respectively. He has worked on several research areas in Counselling, Psychology, Teacher Education and open and distance learning (ODL). He is widely published in nationally and internationally accredited journals. Currently, he is serving on secondment as the Executive Director of the African Council for Distance Education (ACDE), Nairobi, Kenya.

Jude Ssempebwa (PhD) is Associate Professor of Higher Education at the EASHESD, CEES, Makerere University. A holder of a BA (Ed), MA (Ed Mgt) and a PhD of Makerere University, he has taught, researched and/or edited publications at Makerere University, Uganda Management Institute, Uganda Martyrs University, Nkumba University, Kisubi Brothers University College, Kampala International University and the University of KwaZulu-Natal. He is a member of the Organisation for Social Science Research in Eastern and Southern Africa (OSSREA) and American Education Research Association (AERA). He is the editor of Makerere Journal of Higher Education and the founding editor of Uganda Martyrs University Book Series. His research focuses on international higher education in low and middle income countries; the management of educational resources in Sub-Saharan Africa; and the contemporary reform agenda in African Higher Education.

Karim N. A. Ssesanga (PhD) is a lecturer in the Department of Educational Leadership and Management, School of Management Science, Uganda Management Institute (UMI). He is the Head of the Master's in Higher Education Management and Administration programme and the Coordinator of the PhD (Ed. Mgt & Admin.) programme at UMI. He is a Commonwealth Scholar and Higher Education Expert. He holds a PhD in Education Management and Administration from the University of Bristol, United Kingdom.

Lester Brian Shawa (PhD) is a senior lecturer in Higher Education Training and Development at the University of KwaZulu-Natal in Durban, South Africa. He obtained his PhD from Victoria University of Wellington (New Zealand) after finalising an MEd. (Education Policy Studies) with distinction at Stellenbosch University (South Africa). Currently, Dr Shawa is the coordinator of postgraduate studies in Higher Education at the University of KwaZulu-Natal. Prior to his current post, he was the deputy dean of the Faculty of Education at Mzuzu University (Malawi) as well as a research fellow at the School of Education, University of the Witwatersrand (South Africa). He has published in peer reviewed journals and is active in research, touching on higher education policy-praxis, critical theory, international higher education, university pedagogy, citizenship education, deliberative democracy and quality discourses in higher education.

Livingstone Ddungu (PhD) is a lecturer of educational planning at the EASHESD, CEES, Makerere University. A holder of Bachelor's, Master's and PhD degrees from Makerere University, Ddungu has taught and administered at all the levels in Uganda's education system for over thirty-five years and is the recipient of a presidential award for outstanding contribution to the development of education in the country.

Mahmood Mamdani (PhD) is professor and director at Makerere Institute of Social Research (MISR). He received his PhD in government from Harvard University. Mamdani is also Herbert Lehman Professor of Government in the Department of Anthropology and Political Science and the School of International and Public Affairs at Columbia University, where he was also director of the Institute of African Studies from 1999 to 2004. He has taught at the University of Dar es Salaam (1973–79), Makerere University (1980–93), and University of Cape Town (1996–99) and was the founding director of Centre for Basic Research in Kampala, Uganda (1987–96). Mamdani is the author of Good Muslim, Bad Muslim: America, the Cold War and the Origins of Terror; When Victims Become Killers: Colonialism, Nativism and Genocide in Rwanda; Citizen and Subject: Contemporary Africa and the Legacy of Late Colonialism; and ten other books. Mamdani was president of the Council for the Development of Social Research in Africa (CODESRIA) from 1999 to 2002.

Peter Neema-Abooki (PhD) holds a Master's and PhD in Educational Management. He also holds a postgraduate diploma in Education and various qualifications in philosophical and theological disciplines. He is an associate professor of Higher Education at the EASHESD, CEES, Makerere University, where he is also the founding dean. Earlier, he lectured Educational Foundations, Educational Administration, Educational Planning, and Management at Kampala University, Kisubi Brothers' University and Kyambogo University. He is editor-in-chief of the

International Journal of Progressive and Alternative Education. He is also an external examiner in several universities and a member of various professional associations and technical committees.

Philipo Lonati Sanga (PhD) is currently a lecturer in the Department of Educational Foundations, Management and Lifelong Learning of the School of Education, University of Dar es Salaam. He holds a Diploma in Education from Dar es Salaam Teachers' College; a BEd. (Adult Education) and an MA (Education) of the University of Dar es Salaam; and a PhD in Educational Technology of Hanyang University, South Korea. His research focuses on Adult and Community Education; Open, Distance and Flexible Learning; Higher Education; and Assessment for Learning.

Ritah N. Edopu (BIFA, MA [Fine Art], PGD [Mgt]) is a fine artist, lecturer and researcher at Makerere University. She is currently a PhD candidate at the College of Engineering, Design, Art and Technology (CEDAT), Makerere University. Her research focuses on University Community Partnerships, Art Education and Active Learning Methodologies. Ritah is also a painter and has conducted exhibitions in Africa, Europe and US.

Sello E. Moyo is a lecturer in the area of research, statistics and demography at Kanye Seventh Day Adventist College of Nursing where he is also the chairperson of the institution's review board. He is also the country representative for Educational Assessment and Research Network in Africa. A holder of a Master of Education in Research and Evaluation and a BSc in Agricultural Education, Moyo has worked as an agricultural educator, presented at national and international conferences and published articles in the area of teacher education and educational assessment.

Stephen Bolaji (PhD) is a lecturer in the Department of Educational Foundations, Faculty of Education, University of Lagos. He specialises in Philosophy of Education. He is also a member of the Philosophy of Education Association of Nigeria (PEAN).

Vincent Ado Tenebe is a professor at, and the Vice Chancellor of, the National Open University of Nigeria (NOUN) — a position he assumed in October, 2010. Before assuming the leadership of NOUN, he was the pioneer Deputy Vice Chancellor, Administration (2008 – 2010) of the same University. He is a member of the Executive Board of the ACDE, where he also serves as first Vice President. He is also the UNESCO/ COL Professorial Chair in Open and Distance Learning in Nigeria. He has published in several learned journals across the world and he is a member of various learned societies.

Tables

Table 5.1:	Population and Sample	63
Table 5.2:	Distribution of Respondents	65
Table 6.1:	Attributes of Human Capital Developed by the Universities	79
Table 6.2:	Students' Post-Graduation Motives	80
Table 6.3:	Relationships between Attributes of Human Capital Developed and Students' Post-Graduation Motives	82
Table 6.4:	Prediction of Post-Graduation Motives by the Attributes of Human Capital Developed	83
Table 8.1:	Population and Sample	104
Table 8.2:	Perception of the Importance of Intellectual Capital	105
Table 8.3:	Factors Considered in Joining University	106
Table 8.4:	Perception of University Governance Practices	109
Table 8.5:	Perception of Transparency and Disclosure	112
Table 8.6:	Perception of Intellectual Capital Management	114
Table 8.7:	Relationship between Governance and Intellectual Capital	116
Table 9.1:	Level of Agreement that Higher Education Addresses Attributes of Relevance to the Labour Market	122
Table 11.1:	Mean Scores on Attributes of Organisational Commitment	148
Table 11.2:	Reasons Cited for Remaining in Employing University	151
Table 12.1:	ACDE Member Institutions	156
Table 12.2:	Members of the Executive Board of ACDE	158
Table 13.1:	Level to which University of Botswana Teacher Trainees Feel that Teaching is a Stereotyped Occupation	170

Table 13.2: ANOVA in Teacher Trainees' Perception of Teaching and Attitude towards Teacher Training Programme and Teaching 171

Table 13.3: Post Hoc Analysis of Teacher Trainees' Perception of Teaching and Attitude towards Teacher Training Programme and Teaching 172

Acronyms

ACU	Association of Commonwealth Universities
ACDE	African Council for Distance Education
ANSTI	African Network of Scientific and Technological Institutions
AUC	African Union Commission
BRIC	Brazil, Russia, India and China
CBHE	Cross-Border Higher Education
CEES	College of Education and External Studies (Makerere University)
CHE	Commission for Higher Education
CIEFFA	International Centre for Girls' and Women's Education in Africa
CoSN	Consortium for School Networking
CUE	Commission for University Education
EASHESD	East African School of Higher Education Studies and Development
ECOWAS	Economic Community of West African States
EPRC	Education Policy Review Commission
HEIs	Higher Education Institutions
ITEK	Institute of Teacher Education, Kyambogo
MISR	Makerere Institute of Social Research
NCHE	National Council for Higher Education

NIE	National Institute of Education
ODL	Open and Distance Learning
OERs	Open Educational Resources
PDD	Planning and Development Department
R&D	Research and Development
S&T	Science and Technology
SARI	Savannah Agricultural Research Institute
STI	Science, Technology and Innovation
TAI	Technology Achievement Index
TCU	Tanzania Commission for Universities
UACE	Uganda Advanced Certificate of Education
UCE	Uganda Certificate of Education
UDS	University for Development Studies
UOTIA	Universities and Other Tertiary Institutions Act
WHO	World Health Organisation
FDRE	Federal Democratic Republic of Ethiopia
UEA	University of East Africa

Foreword

The thirteen chapters in this book highlight the importance of universities as centres for the generation of knowledge, trainers of skilled workers and creators of the next generation of thinkers. They also emphasise the uniqueness of a university. A university is a multidisciplinary institution that gives space for the search and transmission of all knowledge. Although practical work skills may be delivered in some of its units, a university is not a vocational institute aiming at turning out artisans. A university is concerned with the training of the mind to think, generate ideas, innovate for society and create the next generation of thinkers. To do so effectively, a university needs complete institutional and academic freedom.

The history of Makerere since the 1970 Act was enacted has shown that whenever these twin freedoms are impinged on by internal or external forces, the quality of research and teaching suffers. It is important that oppressive residuals of that infamous Act, which were incorporated into the Universities and Other Tertiary Institutions' Act (UOTIA) of 2001, are repealed.

This book comes at a point when Makerere must decide whether, as Sicherman (2005) put it, "it is a university of Africa or in Africa". Is Makerere a foreign university located in Africa, using foreign theoretical conceptions to teach, analyse issues and train the next generation of academics using imported knowledge? Is Makerere, after 90 years of existence, trying to do original home-based research and locally training its postgraduate students?

Mahmood Mamdani's chapter (seven) deals with this issue aptly. For him, Makerere can only stand up when it adopts a knowledge production model that uses locally generated knowledge and also trains the next generation of academics at home. He feels that the best option for African universities is to locally generate their own knowledge and locally train the next generation of academics in institutions in "which they will have to work" using the best available technology in knowledge creation and dissemination. He advises that "postgraduate education, research and institution building" should be part of a single coin and abhors "the spread of a corrosive consultancy culture". This culture makes African academics mere data collectors whose role is to answer questions set by overseas clients who use the same data to get finished knowledge products for re-export to African universities for use in our lecture rooms. African universities must create their knowledge and train their academics if they are to be "of Africa".

Pursuing the same theme of creating an intellectually based African university, Karim Ssesanga discusses the factors that make a university attract and retain intellectual capital (i.e. brilliant academics). He feels that well governed institutions with good remuneration and facilities for research and training are key to staff attraction and retention. He feels that Makerere's ability to do so will determine its quality. Haruna Yakubu (Chapter 1) follows up the same theme by stating that African universities must use science and technology to generate knowledge, innovate for society and thereby play their true role in African development. He also feels that the role of higher education is not only to train for the market, but also to generate knowledge, innovate and create the next generation of academics.

A number of other issues are discussed in this collection. Philipo Lonati Sanga (Chapter 2) discusses the impact of cross-border higher education and its impact on a university such as Makerere. Although he believes these programmes increase access and affordability, their quality is difficult to determine or regulate. Fred Bakkabulindi discusses the role of an individual in changing university behaviour, tradition and development. He uses William Senteza-Kajubi's impact on the Uganda higher education landscape as an example. Senteza-Kajubi advocated increased access, fairness and the deregulation of Uganda's higher education to permit private universities to operate. Noah, Oni and Bolaji discuss the impact of deregulation (privatisation) of the higher education sector on education quality in Nigeria. They conclude, like many of us in East Africa have done, that privatisation has "had positive and negative outcomes." Although access was expanded, quality was compromised as Mamdani (2007) observed. Ssempebwa, Mulumba and Edopu (Chapter 5) discuss the factors that influence student movements across borders. They point out that, in the East African region, Uganda has had a competitive edge. But "its ability to retain these students and to attract more will depend on the quality" of Ugandan HEIs. Ddungu (Chapter 6) discusses the "attributes of human capital developed by Ugandan universities and students' postgraduate motives". His findings are that knowledge delivered by our universities does not meet students' postgraduate motives, and universities are not responding to the market demands for relevant knowledge and skills. He advises that we should pay attention to "industry-specific knowledge". His chapter, however, does not address the difference between a university and a vocational institution. In Chapter 9, Gebru discusses the responsiveness of Ethiopian universities to the labour market. He feels that there is a mismatch between market demands and what is taught in universities. Teaching in Ethiopian universities is still "traditional"; based on theoretical analysis of known knowledge. In Chapter 10, Lester Brian Shawa discusses the challenges of university governance in Malawi. He briefly points out the impact of neoliberal policies on governance. State interference in the management of universities is one of the major problems impacting on the ability of universities to perform their roles as knowledge producers and disseminators.

These chapters show the problems of defining higher education, particularly what characterises an ideal or Model University for Africa — and in Africa. It is important for us to constantly define what a university is, the nature of the university we would like to have in Africa, and the steps we should take to Africanise the production and content of knowledge for passing on to the next generation of academics in Africa. How long can we continue to import over 80% of the knowledge we use in our textbooks and curricula? The chapters in this volume may not answer all the questions, but they are part of the debate.

A.B.K. Kasozi
Research Associate
Makerere Institute of Social Research
Founding Executive Director NCHE

Preface and Acknowledgements

Founded in 1922 as a technical college enrolling 14 day students of carpentry, building and mechanics, Makerere was started by the British colonial administration in East Africa primarily to address two objectives: produce a middle-level workforce to assist the colonial administration in Eastern Africa and deter completers of secondary of education from seeking higher education in North America and Asia — where they could learn to agitate for political independence upon returning to Africa. Later, citing the unviability of Makerere, recommendations were made for moving the college to Nairobi in Kenya or to Kololo hill in Kampala (if government preferred to retain it in Uganda) except that Sir Philip Euen Mitchell, Governor of Uganda at the time, resisted the recommendations and initiated visionary changes that laid the foundations for Makerere to become the university of international repute it is today.

Despite its lowly beginnings and the aforementioned pessimism, the college developed into notable pre-eminence — especially during what Sicherman (2005) aptly characterises as its "glory years" — affiliating with the University College of London (1949 to 1963) and metamorphosing into part of the University of East Africa in 1963 and into Makerere University in 1970. But, starting the early 1970s, the university also had to contend with serious crises stretching from gross underfunding and unionism through notorious state interference to crippling brain drain and dilapidated infrastructure. It is in responding to these crises that the university implemented the neoliberal reforms of the mid-1980s and revamped several of its subsystems, realising what Court (1999) analogised as a "quiet revolution". Yet, as Mamdani (2007) explains, implementation of these reforms presented daunting dilemmas. Current efforts at the university — including transition to a collegiate system of organisation — are geared towards addressing these and emerging challenges and several rankings suggest that Makerere does not only continue to be Uganda's flagship university, but also a HEI of global pre-eminence.

In 2012, the governing council, management, staff, students and alumni of the university celebrated 90 years of building this pre-eminence, including among other achievements, a large and expanding campus environment; a multidisciplinary undergraduate and postgraduate curriculum; an internationally diverse staff and student body; and globally notable alumni — including heads of government and global thought leaders who are the recipients of prestigious international appointments and felicitations. As part of these celebrations, the principal of the CEES invited the EASHESD to develop and publish a book in the area of higher education management in honour of the university's 90 years of excellence.

Accordingly, the school invited chapter proposals — discussing and contributing ideas for dealing with some of the issues that the university and similar institutions are contending with — in a call for manuscripts that was circulated internationally. The school also established a board of expert reviewers to advise the editors of the book on the relevance, originality, significance, topicality, quality and audience of the submissions received. This was with the view to ensuring that the book is produced at a level of quality that befits the legacy of Makerere University's 90 years of excellence. Sadly, despite an impressive turnout of submissions, the reviewers' comments were against publication of the vast majority of the manuscripts received. Regardless, we are glad that some of the submissions made the mark and that these are as diverse as from Botswana, Ethiopia, Ghana, Kenya, Malawi, Nigeria, Tanzania and Uganda and touching on research and development, internationalisation, access, liberalisation, student affairs, curriculum reform and governance. In his foreword, Professor A.B.K. Kasozi provides a most useful synthesis of the chapters in the book. It is our hope that you find the book a useful resource.

Publication of the book was not without challenges. A particularly long, and sometimes tedious, institutional procurement procedure coupled with the volume of correspondence inherent to double blind peer review significantly delayed production of the book. However, the persevering commitment of various people enabled completion of the project despite these challenges. We thank them for their diligence. Our sincere thanks go to all the authors who responded to our call for manuscripts, published or not. We are also grateful to Professor Fred Masagazi Masaazi, the Principal CEES, for the opportunity to work on this project and for approving funding for the same. Our thanks are also due to the anonymous reviewers who advised on the quality of the manuscripts for their constructive reviews. Dr Ronald Bisaso, the Dean EASHESD; Dr Anthony Muwagga Mugagga, Deputy Principal CEES; past and present staff of the EASHESD, namely,

Dr Beatrice Sekabembe, Dr Catherine Nabayego, Dr David Onen, Dr Edris S. Kasenene, Associate Professor F.E.K. Bakkabulindi, Dr Hillary T. Mukwenda, Dr John Bosco Ssettumba, Dr Joseph Kimoga, Dr Livingstone Ddungu, Dr Robert Kyaligonza, Dr Vincent Owomujuni, Mrs Scovia Ssekweyama, Ms Regina Bisikwa and Mrs Bernadette Kulubya; Mrs Sheila Mwebaze Tindi, the Communication Officer, CEES; Mr Tadeo Ibanda, the Procurement Officer, CEES, and Mr Wamai Mark, Web Manager at Makerere Public Relations, also contributed in various ways towards processes of the project and we thank them. Mr Tom Tibaijuka, Mr Julius Ocwinyo, Mr Julian Treadaway, Mr Kanyemibwa Emma and other staff of Fountain Publishers also provided very useful editorial support and we thank them. Finally, we thank Professor A.B.K. Kasozi for accepting our invitation to write a foreword to the book.

Jude Ssempebwa
Peter Neema-Abooki
J.C.S. Musaazi
EASHESD

Chapter 1

Higher Education for Innovation and Development[1]

Haruna Yakubu

Introduction

Issues at the intersection of higher education, innovation and development might not be topical for much of the developed world because that is what they have been pre-occupied with since the dawn of the industrial age. For them, the relation between science, technology, innovation and higher education has long been well established. For us here in Africa, it is heart-warming that such a linkage is becoming concretised in the scholarly community and industry. The linkage is gradually filtering into the national policy apparatuses of various African countries.

One could actually say that there are two aspects to the topic under discussion. That is, Higher Education for Development, as well as Innovation for Development. Both Higher Education and Innovation are linked to development because they are ways through which the learning of new ideas and the establishment

---

1 This is a slightly edited version of a paper delivered as a keynote address by the author at the Eighth Regional Higher Education Research and Policy Network Conference. The paper is published herein with the kind permission of the author.

of new frontiers of knowledge and progress are registered. It is the diffusion of innovations that are products of sciences and technology research for social good that will ultimately define our national and continental development. It was so for the developed world. It has been so for the BRIC countries and it must be so for our dear Africa. Banking on the promotion of science, technology and innovation through higher education and industry linkages is the tried and tested path to national development.

This chapter will be anchored around two nodes:
- Higher education and national science, technology and innovation research capacity; and
- The communication of innovations.

The linking of science and technology (S&T) with innovation as a policy in many African countries is a recent one. Linking innovation to national development capacity is largely a recent idea in the discourse of national development in most African countries.

Indeed, as recently as between 2000 and 2004, in Ghana, government policy on S&T in relation to national development shied away from the imperative of innovation. Science and technology research was not clearly articulated as the source of innovation for development. So, it was only in 2010 that a new National Science, Technology and Innovation Policy added the innovation factor as an imperative of national development.[2] Why did it take Ghana so long to discover the need for local science and technology research to generate innovations in answer to her national development needs? I want to suggest that this late wake-up call to putting innovation generation and diffusion on

---

2   Ghana Government. (2010). *National Science Technology and Innovation Policy*. Ministry of Environment Science and Technology, Accra. This document is the first policy document in Ghana that articulates science and technology policy within the context of innovation.

the national agenda is a fallout from the type of development paradigm that we put in place as a country in the post-colonial era. This development paradigm called modernisation considered the transfer of science, and technology results from the developed countries to the developing countries as a means to leapfrogging into a developed status.[3] After years of a policy and practice of modernisation and technology transfer, we are beginning to realise the importance of local generation of technological innovations. For me, then, it is heart-warming that the state apparatus in Ghana has recognised the need to widen the focus on Science and Technology to Science, Technology and Innovation, even if belatedly.

Higher Education and National Science, Technology and Innovation Capacity

I think there is no second guessing the significance of higher education to national and continental development. Across the spectrum of state, industry and civil society groups, one easily gets a consensus on the importance of tertiary education. However, this generally accepted belief about higher education looks flimsy upon interrogation. Before doing this interrogation on our continental record on higher education in the last decade or two, let us step back a bit and remind ourselves about the centrality of higher education.

The first point is that higher education is the only avenue for the production of the high calibre human resource required for knowledge generation, through research and experimentation, leading to the creation and adoption of innovation. A National

---

3   Rostow, W.W. (1960). States of economic growth: A non-communist manifesto; Philip McMichael (2000) Development and social change: A global perspective. Thousand Oaks, California: Pine Forge Press.

Association of State Universities and Land-Grant Colleges in the United States working paper states that "tertiary education institutions support knowledge-driven economic growth strategies and poverty reduction by generating new knowledge, building the capacity to access existing stores of global knowledge and adapting that knowledge to local use" (p. 7).[4] It goes on to point out that the basic and applied research work carried out at universities leads to the production of technical innovations, adding that, indeed, "progress in agriculture, health and the environmental sectors, science, engineering and technology is heavily dependent on the application of such innovations" (p. 7).

In the past, universities had to contend with their traditional mandate as being institutions for the generation of knowledge, teaching and occasional service to the community. The production of knowledge through research and peer communication has now given way to a widened mandate. This requires that knowledge itself is not enough until it is translated into a form of benefit or reward for society. Generally, such a transformation occurs through the medium of innovation production and diffusion. That transformation of knowledge into diffusible innovation is central to attempts by universities to be relevant and justify massive public investment. For the developed countries and the BRIC countries, this has been the route through which they have evolved or are evolving a knowledge economy. There is now widespread consensus that knowledge production triggers economic growth.

---

[4] Teshome Yizengaw (2008). "Challenges of higher education in Africa and lessons of experience for the Africa–U.S. higher education collaboration initiative". Working Paper. National Association of State and Land-Grant Colleges, Washington DC.

However, if universities are expected to contribute to national development through research in science, technology and innovation, we should ask ourselves: Is there a role for universities as knowledge producing institutions in national development plans across Africa? This is a question that Cloete et al.[5] asked in their comprehensive study of universities and economic development in Africa. They used a sample of eight African countries (Botswana, Tanzania, Mozambique, Ghana, Uganda, Mauritius, Kenya and South Africa) to undertake the study. Generally, the findings suggest that there is a serious disconnect between authors of national development plans and universities, while several of these countries failed to articulate a serious link between knowledge production as the core business of universities and national development. At best, as knowledge production institutions, universities are focused on national human resource development, and not knowledge for innovation development and diffusion.

This disconnect is a result of the fact that African national development planning institutions are used to the administration of development practice as a modernisation process of technology transfer and foreign dependency. Technology transfer is not an easy solution to development. As Desai et al. have pointed out in their UNDP publication:

> Not all countries need to be on the cutting age of global technological advance. But every country needs the capacity to understand and adapt global technologies for local needs. It is often mistakenly assumed that technology transfer and diffusion are relatively easy, that developing countries can simply import and apply knowledge from outside by

---
5   Nico Cloete, Tracy Bailey, Pundy Pillay, Ian Bunting and Peter Maassen, (2011). Universities and economic development in Africa. Centre for Higher Education Transformation (CHET): South Africa.

obtaining equipment, seeds and pills. But for firms or farms to use a new technology—to identify its potential benefits, to learn it, adapt it and use it—requires new skills and the ability to learn and develop new skills with ease.[6]

Neil Postman on his part has warned us that a new technology "is not additive, it is ecological. A new technology does not just add something, it changes everything."[7] What he sought to point out was that technology is not a value free addition to our lot. It defines our lot and path to the future. And if all that you do is dependent on technology transfer, it sets you up on a path of dependency. Technology transfer can only be helpful to the national development process if it is tied to local capacity generation to complement through research and the generation of useful innovations. This then is the challenge of our time: How do we influence the policy process to shift its gaze from external sources to potential internal sources? In recent times, we have heard arguments for prioritising local content in the oil and gas sector. We should be extending this to local content capacity building in the transfer of technology.

Realising our local capacity in science, technology and innovation generation will depend on the capacity of our HEIs, and our prioritisation of science and engineering education at the tertiary level.

The general state of higher education is one that needs serious attention from governments on the continent. In many global rankings of issues related to higher education, and scholarly and research output, the usual story is that African countries compete

---

6   M. Desai, S. Fukuda-Parr, C. Johansson, and F. Sagast, (2002). Measuring Technology Achievement of Nations and the Capacity to Participate in the Network Age http://hdr.undp.org/en/reports/global/hdr2002/papers/ip_desai-2.pdf

7   Neil Postman (1992) Technopoly, the surrender of culture to technology

from the bottom or are unlisted due to lack of statistical data. And where data is available, the facts are often grim. According to the African Network of Scientific and Technological Institutions (ANSTI, 2003), in several African university departments, only 30% to 40% of required faculty are at post. The average on the continent is 70%. A 2005 ANSTI study of faculty in science and engineering departments in Nairobi, Addis Ababa, Malawi, Lagos, Ahmado Bello, Jomo Kenyatta, Dar es Salaam, Botswana, Ibadan and Cape Coast showed that some 50% of staff had doctoral degrees.[8] Meanwhile, the International Organisation of Migration reported in 2005 that about 40,000 Africans with PhDs lived outside the continent with 10,000 of them being Nigerian academics working in the United States.

Prof. Wisdom Tettey (2006)[9] based in Alberta, Canada reported from his 2006 study that 43% of University of Nairobi faculty and 50% of University of Ghana faculty are over 50 years of age and nearing retirement. In recent times, there has been injection of a crop of younger faculty, but the expansion in higher educational institutions, both public and private, suggests that this trend might not have changed much after six years.

With all these odds against higher education on the continent, how can African universities assert themselves as significant agents in the business of knowledge production and innovation? Generally, research output by way of publications is the measure by which we can rank universities as knowledge production centres. But imagine that the best story in an African university is that faculty research output is at an average of one article published per year per member of the academic staff. Outside South Africa,

---

8 ANSTI 2003, ANSTI 2005.
9 Wisdom Tettey, (2006). "Staff retention in African universities: Elements of a sustainable strategy". Washington DC: World Bank.

Makerere ranks top with an average of one article in every five years. For the rest of Africa, the average comes to one article in every 10 years.[10] Such an abysmal record of research output gives Sub-Saharan Africa a record of contributing only 0.7% of global scientific output.[11]

Ugandan academic, Mahmood Mamdani, in bemoaning the current conditions said, "The global market tends to relegate Africa to providing raw material (data) to outside academics who process it and then re-export their theories back to Africa."[12]

What is the Purpose of Higher Education?

Primarily, higher education leads to an advanced level of understanding in a particular field of knowledge. But above this, it must be a mechanism for learning the tools and methods of producing knowledge. This is a key requirement of higher education, especially graduate training, as it is not just what knowledge you learn while in graduate school, but rather the ability to keep on learning and producing new knowledge long after graduation that is the hallmark of graduate training. Where higher education properly plays this function, education and training become the key drivers of productivity and economic and social development.[13] As has been widely recognised, countries that have consistently invested substantially in higher education and research and development (R&D) have reaped benefits, as is shown in their status as success stories of economic and social

---

10   Cloete et al. 2011
11   Paul Effah and Ivan Addae-Mensah, (2013), "Module on Research and Scholarship: Senior Academic Leadership Training". NCTE, Accra
12   Mahmood Mamdani, (2011). "The importance of research in a university". www.pambazuka.org/en/category/feature/72782/print.
13   Augusto Lopez-Claros and Yasmin N. Mata, (2011). "Policies and Institutions underpinning country innovation: Results from the Innovation Capacity Index".

development. These countries include Japan, Finland, Sweden, Korea, Taiwan and Israel.

The gap between the developed countries and developing countries in terms of investment in R&D relative to their economies is quite high. "For example, the gross domestic expenditure on R&D shares of Sweden and Finland are respectively nearly 400 and 350 times that of Zambia".[14] Most of the African countries do not report their expenditure on R&D. Of the few that report, Zambia spends about 0.01% of its GDP on R&D while Uganda reported highest at 0.74% (excluding South Africa). In Ghana, the 2010 National Science, Technology and Innovation (STI) Policy document wishes to push for 1% of GDP to support STI in the future. Compare this to the fact that the European Union is targeting 3% of GDP investment in R&D. We are speaking here of percentage terms and not absolute terms.

My submission is that given our developmental challenges in Africa, we need to spend more in percentage terms of GDP on R&D if we are to make any progress in maximising the innovative application of science and technology to our everyday lives. While we have not achieved the targeted expenditure of 1% of GDP on R&D yet, it is important to emphasise that 1% is not good enough. Our STI policy entrepreneurs have a huge job to do here. We need to articulate investment in STI as a cost- effective route to national development rather than a bottomless pit to throw money into.

I want to use Ghana as an example here. For several years now, the Savannah Agricultural Research Institute (SARI) has been engaged in the breeding of new varieties of crops and in the

---

[14] Bikas C Sanyal and N. V. Varghese, (2007). Knowledge for the future: research capacity in developing countries. Paris: UNESCO/International Institute for Education Planning (p. 10).

extension of the results to farmers. Farmers have, in turn, been adopting these new drought and disease resistant, high yielding varieties. The country has been a winner in this. However, we have not quantified the financial benefits of SARI's achievements in this area. If we articulated these achievements to policymakers, additional investment in R&D would be seen as financially rewarding to the country. That would then mean that national budgetary allocations to institutions of research and higher education will not be limited to salaries and emoluments. It will be extended to provisions for research.

Nearby SARI's offices is the Nyankpala campus of the University for Development Studies (UDS), where some high impact studies are carried out on using false yam as animal feed for guinea fowls. Providing cheap animal feed is one of the biggest challenges facing meat production. Meanwhile, false yam is a wild crop, growing in abundance across the Savannah regions of Ghana. It is considered to be a nuisance to crop farmers because once false yam shoots start showing up on a piece of arable land, the land becomes difficult to use for economic production. Investing in commercialising the production of animal feed from false yam could have a win-win outcome for all parties involved. It will provide cheap animal feed to livestock farmers, provide relief to crop farmers whose arable lands are being taken over by the wild crop and, in the end, contribute to the national economy.

I think the two cases of crop research at SARI and animal feed research at UDS exemplify what I consider to be the biggest challenge facing STI policy entrepreneurs. How do we quantify the economic benefits of innovations borne out of research? How do we translate that quantification into monetary terms to make sense to the policymaker? This is how we can demonstrate that investing in STI research at higher educational institutions results in generous returns.

Investment in R&D is directly related to investment in higher education, graduate training and research. Failing to invest in R&D, higher education, and graduate training in science and engineering will mean that African universities will continue to lag behind. This current situation of poor research output[15] means that African universities have become centres of knowledge consumption rather than knowledge production. By this I mean that with virtually no research budgets, no national granting councils to apply to, and low levels of support from the private sector, African universities are restricted to their teaching mandate. Inevitably, it is the knowledge produced from non-African research output that is being used in our classrooms and libraries.

Foundation for Capacity Building

Every now and then, we hear political actors and members of civil society bemoan the fact that our universities and polytechnics produce a disproportionately low number of graduates in science and engineering. It is true that universities and polytechnics may be overproducing graduates in social sciences and humanities. But the issue does not rest with universities and polytechnics alone to resolve. These institutions depend on the categories of candidates that come from the feeder institutions of second cycle schools, whose abilities are also determined by the level of investment in science education that governments are ready to commit. Investing in science education at the secondary level will ultimately produce the right numbers for tertiary institutions to admit.

---

15   Africa contributes only 0.7% to the global scientific output.

African governments that want to reverse the current situation of a disproportionately large number of graduates from social sciences and humanities should start with a commitment to ensuring that a large proportion of all second cycle students are science majors. This will mean that when admissions to the universities are being carried out, there will be enough science and engineering prospects.

The second step will be to make a bold commitment to investing in the science and engineering capacities of universities. With a few exceptions, privately sponsored universities are unable to meet the high financial requirement of investments in science and engineering programmes. As a result, they are often focused on offering programmes in the arts, humanities and business. It is left only to African governments to come up with innovative mechanisms for increasing investment in science and engineering education at the second cycle and tertiary levels of education.

We should avoid the tendency to over-rely on donor support to finance higher education. It is not sustainable. A sustainable approach is to tie it to a percentage levy of major economic activities and put it in a dedicated fund. An example of tying a percentage levy to a major economic activity is the Economic Community of West African States (ECOWAS) levy that importers pay when they bring certain types of goods into ECOWAS countries. A similar levy could be used to support higher educational capacity building.

Communication of Science and Technology Innovation

Research output in science and technology alone is not enough. I have already pointed out that knowledge must be tied to the production of useful innovations, and then diffused to social ends before we can begin to reckon in full the value of the knowledge so produced. That is why I want to emphasise that the communication of science and technology innovation must be of prime importance to scientists as well. The days of limiting our work to peer level communication through journal publications only are over. Scientific journal publication is the first step to authenticate the work. But moving beyond that level is now a requirement for all scientists if society is to appreciate the value for money being expended on them. I have already mentioned the work of SARI and UDS Nyankpala.

It is instructive to note that African countries, as in other global rankings, fare badly in the global Technology Achievement Index (TAI). The index aims to capture technological achievements of a country in four dimensions:

- Creating new technology;
- Diffusing the adoption of new technologies;
- Diffusion of long existing technologies that are still basic inputs into the industrial and network age; and
- Building a human skill base for technological creation and adoption.

The focus of TAI on outcomes and achievements puts premium not just on knowledge production, but on adopted useful innovations borne out of research (Human Development Report 2001 p. 46).[16] TAI ranking is based on composite calculation mechanism. While such a methodology does have its problems, it is reasonably reliable in giving us a true picture of our situation.

Several scholarly and industry attempts have been made at defining what innovation is. From science and technologies studies to agricultural extension, from medicine to cultural

---

16 Human Development Report: "Making new technologies work for human development". UNDP/Oxford University Press, New York 2001.

studies, one gets variations in the definition. What is common to most of these definitions is the emphasis that the idea, process, or product identified as an innovation must be characterised as new to the social system to which it is being introduced. The working definition for this presentation is borrowed from Everett Rogers (2003) who put it that,

> ...an innovation is an idea, practice, or object that is perceived as new by an individual or other unit of adoption. It matters little, so far as human behaviour is concerned, whether or not the idea is 'objectively' new as measured by the lapse of time since its first use or discovery.[17]

Rogers' definition is done within the context of innovation diffusion studies. And that is why this definition is instructive. The relevance of innovation to development depends on its adoption. It is only when an innovation is being adopted that we can begin to reckon its significance to development.

Communicating innovations, ensuring their adoption, as well as communicating the significance of the work of the scientist to other stakeholders in national development are very important dimensions of the work of scientists that have not been given proper attention. Often, scientists are not good at telling their own success stories. Presenting findings in a matter-of-fact manner is not necessarily the same as translating one's work into the language that key stakeholders such as policymakers understand. Our scientists might have mastered the professional art of peer–to–peer communication. It is the fine art of popular communication and stakeholder communication that we need to build upon. In this regard, we need a paradigm shift in our education of scientists to

---

[17] Everett M. Rogers, (2003). Diffusion of Innovation. 5th Edition. New York: Free Press (p. 12).

include training in communication skills. The onset of the digital communication platforms has engendered new types of literacies that have now become a "must-have" skill set for actors in the STI research community.

The traditional academic setting of researching and publishing in peer forums such as books and journals is still most relevant. There is no doubt about that. But the academic researcher, or knowledge production worker of today, is in a new milieu that is far from his/her predecessor. Walter Ong (2002)[18] reminds us that it was the then new technology of print that 'technologised' the world, and gave us the book as the principal medium of the pre-digital age and defined our academic culture with the mandate of producing knowledge. In the last 20 years, computer-mediated communication has become the common platform for producing and sharing knowledge. This transformation has given rise to new types of literacies that STI researchers must have before they can properly function in the digital era. Some of these include: computer literacy, information literacy, visual literacy, and media literacy.

Brill, Kim and Branch (2001) define visual literacy as:

> A group of acquired competencies for interpreting and composing visible messages. A visually literate person is able to: (a) discriminate, and make sense of visible objects as part of a visual acuity; (b) create static and dynamic visible objects effectively in a defined space; (c) comprehend and appreciate the visual testaments of others; and (d) conjure objects in the mind's eye.[19]

---

18 Walter J Ong, (2002). Orality and literacy: Technologizing of the word. London: Routledge.
19 Brill, J.M., Kim, D. and Branch, R.M., (2001). "Visual literacy defined: the results of a Delphi study - Can IVLA (operationally) define visual literacy?" In

The skill-sets that define these literacies are not exclusive to each other. For instance, visual literacy can sometimes be seen as part of information literacy, while media literacy can be seen as encompassing all the other literacies. Increasingly, these competencies are becoming basic requirements for researchers. Teaching now requires a familiarity with various types of literacies.

In view of these, I want to suggest that our academic programming for the training of our future researchers should incorporate the acquisition of these literacies as part of the training process. In the past, a discovery had to wait to be brought to the light of the day through a snail-paced academic publishing system before it could be re-packaged for popular readership. Today, an innovative researcher-blogger can actually build a popular community of interest around his or her work before it travels through the academic publishing mill. It is this popular community of interest that can translate into policy discourse, leading to increased budgetary allocation from principal sponsors such as governments.

For instance, in Ghana, I am still not sure if our policymakers have been properly informed about the work of SARI and UDS Nyankpala on how these innovations have contributed to increasing national food production. But definitely, the global scholarly communities in food crop and animal sciences have been informed through the academic press. Can we imagine for a moment the change if these researchers had social media skills and were blogging and uploading video clips of the socioeconomic transformations that their works are bringing to the rural communities of the Savannah? This would transform

---

R. E. Griffen, V. S. Williams & J. Lee (Eds.), Exploring the visual future: Art design, science and technology. (pp. 9-15) Blacksburg, VA: The International Visual Literacy Association.

their function and bring the benefits of research to the attention of planners and funders.

Conclusion

I want to conclude on the note of emphasising that translating STI information and knowledge for popular consumption is a "must-have" skill that we need to provide to our researchers. The social media front is a frontier that we should consider as equally important as the peer level academic journal publication. Recognising the acquisition of media literacy as part of the vocation of STI researcher will allow for effective diffusion of innovation and assure the taxpayer that his or her money is being put to good use. Policy makers and policy executors will also discover the important work of STI researchers and will find innovative ways of funding our work. The communicative dimension of STI is being underscored here precisely because our STI capacity is tied to the quantum of resource allocation for the sector. We need to find a way to tell our story to stakeholders in Africa. And no other group can tell it better than a well-trained STI researcher.

I also want to remind us that the link between science and technology, on the one hand, and innovation, on the other, is communication. I showed how, in Ghana, the shift from science and technology to science, technology and innovation as part of our national development trajectory moved the work of the scientist from a recluse academic to that of a development worker. The hitherto recluse academic might have mastered his or her work as a knowledge producer but the era of talking science, technology and innovation means that the STI researchers in Africa have to be engaged in our various national development discourse as pivotal players. This is how higher education can speak strongly to national development.

Chapter 2

Challenges and Opportunities for Quality Assurance of Cross-Border Higher Education in East Africa

Philipo Lonati Sanga

Introduction

Cross-border higher education (CBHE) "is a multifaceted phenomenon which includes the movement of people (students and faculty), providers (HEIs with a physical and/or virtual presence in a host country), and academic content (such as the development of joint curricula)" (International Association of Universities et al., 2005, p.6). Due to a number of factors, interest in this approach to higher education development and delivery is growing in many countries. These factors include changes in the composition of student population and student mobility (Organisation for Economic Co-operation and Development, 2004); staff and programme mobility; long distance educational delivery and the global trend of massification of higher education. Other forces behind the significance of CBHE are the nation's increasing awareness on the role that CBHE can play in building national capacity and enhancing regional and global collaborations

(Moore & Lambert, 1996); increased demand for higher and continuing education; and the role of ICT in delivering education.

Many HEIs consider CBHE as a strategic approach to cultivate collaborations; assist receiving nations in human resource development; generate revenue; and respond to the global demand for an educated workforce and a globalised society (Chetro-Szivos, 2010). Besides being an opportunity for both receiving and providing nations, CBHE poses several challenges to the education sector. Due to a nation's incapacity to satisfy the educational demands of all students, there is a general belief that various forms of CBHE can offer better opportunities for improving the skills and competencies of students from the receiving country (Vincent-Lancrin & Pfotenhauer, 2012) than solely relying on domestically supplied education. For instance, while exporting institutions and nations gain from expanding student enrolment and income through tuition fees, importing nations benefit by supplementing the domestic supply of education and gain an educational alternative for their population. On the other hand, a significant challenge in programme mobility is to determine who awards the course credits or final credentials for the programme. Perhaps more important is to find out whether or not the qualifications are credible or recognised for employment or lifelong learning in the receiving country and elsewhere.

In East Africa, the re-establishment of the East African Community, on November 30, 1999, created an opportunity through which CBHE would be more officially promoted and executed within the signatory countries. Although there is a high level of interaction among the East African countries in terms of higher education, they still need more rigorous collaborations among themselves. Besides, the liberalisation of campuses of public universities and globalisation have compelled these countries to promote the role of private universities and distance education to meet the rapidly growing demand for higher education. Of course, this is a global trend.

This chapter presents a few challenges and opportunities for quality assurance in CBHE in East Africa. The new East African Community consists of Burundi, Kenya, Rwanda, South Sudan, Tanzania and Uganda. This chapter focuses on cases from Kenya, Tanzania, and Uganda. These are the member countries of the former East African Community and they are the countries with the most well established and coordinated higher education systems within the Community. However, we must hasten to admit that CBHE in East Africa is still at its infancy stage. As a result, it is a serious challenge to find any useful statistics on its state in any of these three countries. This chapter is expected to provoke the educators' and researchers' interests in this borderless educational delivery from East Africa and elsewhere.

Rationale for Cross-Border Higher Education

CBHE includes higher education that takes place when students follow a course or programme of study that has been produced, and is continuing to be maintained, in a country different from the one in which they are dwelling (Knight, 2007; Uvalic-Trumbic, 2008). Cross-border higher education is sometimes referred to as transnational education or borderless education. Being one manifestation of globalisation, reasons for the emergence of CBHE include changing demographics among nations; substantial growth of student populations worldwide; movement to lifelong learning and the expansion of knowledge economy; and the ICT revolution. Other reasons are the inability of national systems to offer educational opportunities to all and the global demand for internationally acceptable knowledge-based competencies. These considerations culminated in the reality that national sovereignty over higher education is reinforced by the General Agreement on Trade in Services (GATS) of the World Trade Organisation (Knight, 2006). Thus, higher education has been closely aligned with business and economic development of nations. At this juncture, it seems legitimate to question whether HEIs will persistently preserve their missions and visions to execute their core functions.

Benefits of and Threats to Cross-Border Higher Education

CBHE has a number of benefits to both the receiving and the providing country. For instance, the cooperating institutions, teaching staff and students benefit from the cross-fertilisation of knowledge, skills and cultures thereby fostering human understanding across borders. Further, CBHE boosts national educational demands to attain an international dimension of research and teaching and hence institutional quality improvement. Njuguna and Itegi (2013) accurately comment that such regional networks give countries strength to compete on a global arena. This is particularly important in this globalisation era when we witness African countries being deeply engaged in pursuing the Western type of development, sometimes without consideration of their local contexts.

The cross-border mode of delivery creates not only opportunities for knowledge and technology exchange and transfer and the promise to penetrate new markets, but also stimulates competition for scarce resources, especially human capital. However, the practicality of knowledge and technology exchange is usually disturbing due to the inequalities that are likely to emerge between partners. In this situation, the role of governments becomes crucial in providing the necessary structures and procedures that harmonise and strengthen international bonds.

Further, this mode of delivery has several threats; not only to the provider but also the receiver. For instance, although it is generally claimed that CBHE offers an opportunity for a choice of high quality courses, deep inequalities tend to exist (Knight, 2006) between the participating countries. A few countries may dominate the global scientific system and unfortunately new technologies are basically owned by multinational academic institutions from major developed countries. This makes most of East African countries dependent on major academic superpowers. Furthermore, the absence of vibrant regional quality assurance and accreditation mechanisms in East Africa imposes quality risks such as selling and buying of fake degrees which educe a negative impression of cross-border education. It is against such situations that some institutions decide to introduce courses both online and offline through compulsory attendance mode for distance learners.

Quality Assurance for Higher Education in East Africa

Each university in East Africa has some sort of quality assurance mechanism in the form of regulations and criteria of academic staff recruitment and appraisal, rules and regulations on academic activity performance, student evaluations of course delivery, stakeholder involvement in the curriculum review process, external examination systems, and academic auditing as conducted by some universities (Nkunya, 2008). Besides individual universities' own quality assurance mechanisms, there are national educational quality assurance agencies for each country.

At the university level, the first accreditation agency in Africa was Kenya's Commission for Higher Education which was established in 1985 by an Act of Parliament, the Universities Act Cap 210B (National Council for Law Reporting, 2012). This Commission started as a result of public concerns about the quality of higher education and the existence of several institutions offering "university education whose establishment and development was uncoordinated and unregulated" (Hayward, 2006, p. 12). Among its functions were accreditation and inspection of institutions of higher education. The real accreditation process began in 1989 in Kenya only for private universities. Among the first to be accredited was the Catholic University of East Africa. Accreditation in Kenya is now a requirement for private universities, public universities other than those established by an Act of Parliament, foreign universities, and any other agency operating on behalf of any of those institutions. The Commission for Higher Education was succeeded by the Commission for University Education (CUE) with effect from 2012.

In Tanzania, the Higher Education Accreditation Council which had been in operation since 1995 was then succeeded by the Tanzania Commission for Universities (TCU) beginning on July 1, 2005. Previously, all universities and non-university HEIs implemented their obligatory functions as set forth in their individual Acts of Parliament or constitutions including the development of internal quality assurance systems. The TCU is entrusted to recognise, approve, register, and accredit universities and university colleges (both campus and distance modes of delivery) operating in Tanzania and local or foreign university-level programmes being offered by non-registered HEIs (TCU, 2010). This Commission also coordinates the proper functioning of all university institutions in Tanzania so as to foster a harmonised higher education system in the country. In order to ensure that such a harmonious higher education system does not compromise institutional peculiarities and autonomy, each university has the legal right to operate under its own charter.

Having realised the truth that global forces are transforming the way higher education is being delivered, Uganda sought to set up a regulatory body for higher education. Thus, the NCHE was established in 2001 by the UOTIA (Republic of Uganda 2001). This is a semi-autonomous and self-accounting body. The core mission of this agency is to set standards and regulations to ensure that all public and private tertiary education institutions in Uganda create, sustain, and provide relevant and quality higher education for all qualified Ugandans and to meet the local and global higher education challenges of the future.

Like many other places around the world, the guidelines for quality assurance as stipulated by the TCU, the CUE, and the NCHE have many similarities. In general, except for the variations in nomenclature, the higher education quality assurance agencies in these three countries insist on similar core standards and indicators for quality assurance. Nevertheless, there are few standards and guidelines which seem to be unique to each country. For instance, while the NCHE of Uganda specifies physical resources, the CUE of Kenya and the TCU focus on facilities in general. Further, the TCU and the NCHE highlight the campus size as a separate issue which counts when assessing quality of higher education. Understandably, campus size may be an issue of concern for conventional and dual modes of delivery but not necessarily a factor to consider for cross-border educational delivery.

Common components of institutional quality assurance guidelines in East Africa are: Institutional objectives, mission and vision; strategic planning; institutional governance; academic character or orientation; academic programmes or curricula on offer; quality of teaching and learning; human resource and academic staffing; availability and quality of facilities such as library services and the extent of mobilisation and management of financial resources.

Challenges in Implementing Cross-Border Higher Education in East Africa

Although I have described earlier the general threats to cross-border higher education (CBHE), in this section, I intend to provide a detailed discussion on the challenges that are encountered specifically by the East African countries as they engage in implementing CBHE.

Establishing and managing quality assurance for both incoming and outgoing educational programmes is not an easy task. Despite the strengths of mutual collaboration for provision and quality assurance of higher education, East African countries face a number of challenges related to regional implementation of CBHE.

International Challenges: The Global North Hegemony

In this context, the Global North consists of countries which are mainly former colonial powers and the Global South consists of formerly colonised countries which include all East African countries. Some authors call the Global North Developed Countries or First World Countries and the Global South Developing Countries or Third World Countries. What is clear is that quality assurance in higher education is increasingly becoming a global venture positioned in a field characterised by significant asymmetries (Ramirez, 2014). Belonging to countries of the Global South, HEIs in East Africa are predominantly prone to uncritically adopt approaches to quality assurance applied in the Global North. This is due to the fact that the diffusion of ideas and educational reform practices is progressively unidirectional, from the North to the South. Certainly, one is compelled to question who establishes international standards for quality and who benefits from such diffusion.

The most likely possibility of engaging in the implementation of CBHE at a wider international perspective is for the East African countries to experience a widening gap between themselves as losers and the North as winners. For instance, the United States of America, followed by Europe, have been regarded as the main exporters of accreditation and quality assurance guidelines and standards (Jackson, Davis & Jackson, 2010). As a result, there is an extrinsic desire of every institution to become world class – a phenomenon which is contentious but powerful and pervasive. Universities and other higher learning institutions are investing heavily in marketing and branding campaigns in order to acquire name recognition and to boost enrolments. Whether internationalisation of quality assurance of higher education promotes collaboration and joint problem-solving or exacerbates competition and power struggles depends on individual country's preparedness for globalisation. Whereas the Global North seems to depict aggressive competition, the East African countries are typically passive recipients of global ideas from the North. Thus, under such global power differences between the North and the South, CBHE can be used as a tool for perpetuating those differences instead of levelling the playing field.

Regional challenges: Intra and inter-national challenges

New technologies have been influential in increasing accessibility to education and have opened new avenues for cross-border education. Due to advancements in ICT, collaboration in providing and managing quality higher education is sometimes regarded as irrelevant because ICT facilitates an unrestricted penetration of knowledge and technology across borders. In addition, East African countries have different ICT policies and they certainly differ in the levels at which they have integrated technology in education. These differences may have some implication on the extent of harnessing the benefits of cross-border higher education (CBHE). Reliable ICT infrastructure will normally create a favourable environment for easy export and import of CBHE.

Agencies of quality assurance in the East African countries delineate the roles played by, for instance, the national governments, professional and academic bodies and student bodies too passively as compared to other international guidelines and standards such as OECD and UNESCO's joint guideline as outlined in Uvalic-Trumbic (2008). This is a challenge because quality assurance of education is a shared responsibility among many stakeholders ranging from student bodies to national governments.

Despite the similarities that exist in many aspects, the general education systems and national educational philosophies of the three countries are different in certain fundamental aspects. For illustration, Tanzania and Uganda follow a 7-4-2-3 system in which there are seven years of primary education, six years of secondary education (divided into four years of ordinary or lower secondary and two years of advanced secondary school) and at least three years of higher education. Kenya follows an 8-4-4 system, which is eight years of primary education, four years of secondary education and at least four years of higher education. These differences have a direct repercussion on student exchange across these countries. Sometimes, students are compelled to do either a bridging programme or a matriculation examination before they are admitted for university studies in a neighbouring country. Under these circumstances, quality of education may mean different things to different institutions and partner countries.

Autonomy and the powers of national accrediting agencies are not uniform across these countries. There is a notable proximity between universities and national structures of power which in East African situations has occasionally tended to curtail academic freedom and intellectual expansion among students and staff. There are several cases of serious government encroachment on university recruitment and renewal of professors' contracts, university budgets, and institutions' administrative procedures in general (Sifuna, 2012). It is further supported by Sifuna (2012, p.127) that although the governments are gradually withdrawing from supporting higher education, their political influence on management of higher education is still notable. Additionally, the incongruity of national quality assurance systems among themselves creates another challenge. As an illustration, Kenya's Commission for University Education (CHE) describes the standards (provider's commitment, design of curriculum, instruction, and course materials, development, staff support, student support, evaluation and assessment, and advertising) and procedures for quality assurance of open and distance learning programmes (CHE, 2008) while Tanzania's and Uganda's agencies are silent about it. Tanzania and Uganda apply the same procedures and standards for both conventional and open and distance learning programmes.

In some cases, institutions and governments are worried that student mobility and foreign education could lead to displacement of local students by international students (Njuguna & Itegi, 2013). Likewise, CBHE tends to cater for an affluent market. That is why most students seeking it are privately sponsored, implying that students from poor economic backgrounds are technically deprived of it.

Institutions may cheat and provide exaggerated data to regional and international agencies on what they offer so as to gain the desired recognition. This challenge is in line with Sum's (2005) view that HEIs are likely to provide exaggerated information about, for example, course/programme content and their delivery and claims on the local recognition of the same. Arguably, pressure from ranking systems of universities and advocacy for global competition are among the accelerating factors for the provision of exaggerated data. Every university is struggling to become "a world class university" (Ramirez, 2014) literally by any means.

Liberalisation policies of education have resulted in a rapid proliferation of HEIs, especially the private ones. Nations are witnessing a huge increase in the launching of universities and the transformation of existing non-degree offering colleges into universities. In my view, some of these institutions are not worthy of university status. Coupled with massification, whereby the numbers of the students surpass the available infrastructure, effective management of higher education is definitely at a crossroads. The problem of degree mills (HEIs that churn out graduates albeit without much regard for the relevance and quality of their educational attainment) has thus become one critical concern of higher education quality assurance agencies in this region.

Opportunities of Implementing Cross-Border Higher Education in East Africa

The ensuing section is prepared to provide a brief analysis of opportunities of implementing cross-border higher education (CBHE) in East Africa. Quality assurance of CBHE by single-country initiatives is clearly cumbersome unless combined efforts from neighbouring countries are implemented. The discussed challenges notwithstanding, East African countries have certain opportunities which, if wisely tapped, the quality of received and provided CBHE may be guaranteed.

In 2006, the three East African higher education regulatory agencies: Kenya's Commission for Higher Education (CHE), the NCHE in Uganda and Tanzania's Commission for Universities (TCU) signed a memorandum of cooperation in a bid to streamline and harmonise higher education accreditation, quality assurance practices and procedures in the region (Buchere, 2009). A harmonised quality assurance system for East Africa, currently being developed, would help to ensure the standards and comparability of CBHE among member countries. Successful development of an East African Quality Assurance Framework would be a yardstick to ensure that university graduates in member countries attained the skills and competencies needed to be relevant to and competitive for jobs in the region and globally. Nonetheless, many years have passed without any substantial progress in developing the envisaged quality assurance framework. Concerted efforts should be made to ensure a more practical progress towards a full scale implementation of regional quality assurance mechanism.

The recent political will of government leaders of East African countries to invigorate a strong East African Community is a great opportunity to expand cooperation in political, economic, socio-cultural and, of course, educational sectors. Following this revival of the East African Community, many HEIs are intensifying their ties across the region. This is a unique opportunity for HEIs to work together and sustain their role as think tanks within the region. More significantly, some top government leaders and educational experts have been passionately advocating a harmonised system of provision and monitoring of higher education in East Africa.

The most prominent public universities of East African countries (Dar es Salaam in Tanzania, Makerere in Uganda and Nairobi in Kenya) have a long, shared and rich history. With their common history and multiple perspectives, they can share their knowledge to address the regional educational issues with a collective voice. It may be of interest to note that, towards the end of 2013, these universities jointly celebrated the start of the University of East Africa (UEA) at Makerere University. At the occasion, a permanent monument, a bust, was unveiled at Makerere for the first and only Chancellor of the UEA, the late Mwalimu Julius Kambarage Nyerere. These universities have the potential to provide leadership in offering high quality higher education at lower cost and less 'restrictive residency model' (Chetro-Szivos, 2010) to promote CBHE within the region. Despite the growing importance of the role of private higher education, public universities still deserve the leadership position in the provision of higher education because, compared to private universities, public universities are more directly monitored by the state (e.g. through appointment of university leaders, payment of staff and provision of regulatory instruments) and the public has greater opportunity to critique the quality of their service delivery.

Conclusion

The global trend of higher education programme and student mobility signifies the reality that provision of cross-border higher education (CBHE) is increasingly becoming imperative in East Africa. Cross-border higher education has the potential to help countries provide accessible and affordable higher education to their citizens. However, CBHE is still making a negligible contribution to the provision of accessible and affordable higher education. The possible limitations to its effectiveness include: low level of technology used in delivery of education, poor and inadequate infrastructure and ineffective national government policies and priorities.

Whether CBHE providers are viewed as competitors or collaborators, or as opportunities or risks, depends on a country's ability to develop appropriate policies and regulations to integrate foreign providers into a national higher education system which is capable of meeting social, cultural, and economic goals. Member institutions and countries need to realise that, despite their many similarities, the goals of higher education and quality assurance systems should be relevant to the respective country's circumstances.

Equally significant, quality assurance of CBHE in East Africa has to be assessed to determine the extent of its juxtaposition to other international guidelines and standards such as those stipulated by OECD and UNESCO (Uvalic-Trumbic, 2008). This is necessary because globalisation pressure poses a paradox of cooperation and competition (Sanga, 2012). Our contemporary era seemingly emphasises the benefits of competition. By sheer scale, however, we cooperate far more often than we compete. Then, the crucial challenging task for institutional and national educational leaders is to strike the balance between the need for cooperation and competition among their respective institutions and nations. If East African countries and HEIs perceive globalisation as an avenue for international cooperation to promote quality improvement in higher education, then careful attention ought to be paid to the ensuing aspects. Concentrate on quality for improvement as opposed to quality for accountability; recognise that quality is contextual; develop a reliable regional model of quality which does not necessarily conform to any international model; and realise that global power differences exist and CBHE can be one tool for perpetuating such differences.

Chapter 3

William Senteza-Kajubi as a Change Agent in Uganda's Education System with Specific Reference to Widening Access to University Education

Fred E. K. Bakkabulindi

Introduction

In this chapter, I examine the life of William Senteza-Kajubi (1926–2012), formerly a Professor of Higher Education, as a change agent in Uganda's education system. In particular, I highlight his contribution to widening access to university education.

Rogers (2003) defines a change agent as an "individual who influences clients' innovation-decisions in a direction deemed desirable by a change agency" (p. 366). He goes on to observe that many different occupations fit that definition: teachers, consultants, public health workers, agricultural extension agents, development workers, and sales people. "All these change agents provide a communication link between a resource system with some kind of expertise and a client system" (p. 368). Rogers also defines another term which seems synonymous with a "change agent", namely "champion". He defines a "champion" as a "charismatic individual who throws his or her weight behind an innovation, thus overcoming indifferences or resistance that the new idea may provoke in an organisation" (p. 414).

Stuart, Mills and Remus (2009) define champions as individuals who emerge to take creative ideas and bring them to life; who actively and enthusiastically promote an innovation, building support, overcoming resistance and ensuring that the innovation is implemented.

Rogers (2003) asserts that "the presence of an innovation champion contributes to the success of an innovation in an organisation" (p. 414). This is so because the change agent functions as a communication link between two or more social systems, playing several roles in the change process. These roles include:

- Developing a need for change on the part of clients;
- Establishing a change relationship with them;
- Diagnosing client problems; and
- Creating intent to change in the client(s) and translating this intent into action.

Leading change is one of the most important and difficult leadership responsibilities (Yukl, 2006). "The role of leadership at all levels of an organization...is paramount for spearheading innovation as a process and maintaining its momentum until innovation... occurs" (Crossan & Apaydin, 2010, p. 1156). Thus, it is important for managers to understand the reasons for, and the nature of, resistance against change and to adopt a clearly defined strategy for the initiation of change (Mullins, 2010).

Change management can be subdivided into two approaches: planned and unplanned. Planned change is a deliberate, premeditated move to alter an organisation's status. It is a change that is initiated and implemented by change leaders to either solve problems, adapt to changes or influence future changes. On the other hand, unplanned change is not sequential. Rather, it is chaotic and often involves shifting of goals, discontinuation of activities and making of unexpected combinations of changes. Nevertheless, for any change process to be successful, it must be properly managed.

In this chapter, I consider Senteza-Kajubi as an education leader who, true to the foregoing theoretical propositions, served as a change manager in Uganda's education system, especially in the area of widening access to university education.

Who was Senteza-Kajubi?

Senteza-Kajubi was born on December 24, 1926 to Yoweri Bugonzi Kajubi and Bulanina Namukomya of Busega, Kampala. He studied at Mackay Memorial Primary School, Nateete, Kampala (1933–1940) and Mengo Junior School in Kampala (1941–1942). Senteza-Kajubi's calling in the early years was to be an agriculturalist, until his Head teacher at Mengo Junior School, Yofesi Y. B. Sempala, advised him to become a teacher. Shortly after, Sempala secured for him a vacancy at King's College Budo, an elitist senior school.

Senteza-Kajubi stayed at Budo for four years (1943–1946) after which he proceeded to Makerere College, now Makerere University, where he studied Geography and Education (1947–1950). Senteza-Kajubi (2004, pp. 4–5) narrates how elitist and exclusive the Makerere College of his time was, saying that:

> Makerere College was at the apex of higher education in the whole of Eastern and Central Africa. It produced the... elite leaders of the future for the entire Region. Teaching

and learning at Makerere at that time was not only a rare privilege, but also a great joy. It was almost a passport to heaven here on earth.

Moreover, he later went to the University of Chicago — another elitist HEI — to do an MA in Geography (1952–1955), as the first African Fulbright scholar (Nakyondwa, 2007).

Upon completion at Makerere College, Senteza-Kajubi embarked on teaching, starting at Kako Junior School in Masaka, in southern Uganda (1951–1952), and later, after his MA, at King's College Budo (Nakyondwa, 2007). At the end of 1958, in what McGregor (2007, p. 152) described as a great loss to Buddo, Senteza-Kajubi was appointed to teach "Methods of teaching Geography in secondary schools" at Makerere University College.

In 1964, Senteza-Kajubi became the Director of the National Institute of Education (NIE). Domiciled at Makerere, the institute was responsible for the development of curricula, examination and certification of primary school teachers and also started the Grade V teachers' course to train non-graduate secondary school teachers.

In 1977, he was appointed the Vice Chancellor of Makerere University, a position he occupied until 1979. Thereafter, he became a Professor of Higher Education at the same university. Ssekamwa (2008) reports that, as a Professor for Higher Education, he worked hard to establish a Department of Higher Education [now the EASHESD]...whose mandate was to design and promote a programme which should induct university lecturers and professors in teaching at university and... other tertiary institutions" (Ssekamwa, 2008, p. 7).

From 1986 to 1990, he was the Principal of the Institute of Teacher Education Kyambogo (ITEK) during which time he also chaired the Education Policy Review Commission (EPRC) (1987–1989). Then, he became the Vice Chancellor of Makerere University for a second time (1990–1993). Thereafter, he led Nkumba University as the Vice Chancellor (1995–2008).

Purpose

The purpose of this paper is two-fold. First, to highlight the fact that although he was a product of a rather elitist education system and in which he eventually served as a teacher and administrator, Senteza-Kajubi was never blind to the unfairness of such a system. Second, to highlight his efforts to widen access to university education in Uganda.

Method

I base the paper on a study in which I took a qualitative approach to collecting data. In particular, I used a phenomenological and longitudinal design, relying on documentary evidence on Senteza-Kajubi, which I deliberately gathered between 1992 and 2012. These data included the speeches he gave; policy documents produced by educational institutions under his stewardship; the interviews he gave to newspapers; the papers he presented at conferences; and the journal articles he authored.

Regarding the order of presentation, I borrowed the words Senteza-Kajubi (2004) used in his introduction. "Where shall we begin, please your Majesty?" Asked one of the characters in Alice's Wonderland, "Begin at the beginning", the King said gravely, "and go on till you come to the end: then stop" (p. 2). As I considered doing this, I chanced upon the introductory remarks to the Third Commencement Lecture of Nkumba University in 2002 (Rubadiri, 2002, p. 1) where Senteza-Kajubi observed that,

In the foreword to a book published in 1919, John Dewey after his first visit to Japan said that anyone who had enjoyed the unique hospitality of Japan would be overwhelmed with confusion if he [sic] endeavoured to make an acknowledgement in any way commensurate to the kindness received.

While I considered it a pleasure and great honour to highlight Senteza-Kajubi's contribution to widening access to university education in Uganda, I became afraid that I would be overwhelmed with confusion if I endeavoured to write an exhaustive paper in any way commensurate with the brilliant and distinguished record of his immense contribution. But at the same time, not trying at all would be an injustice to history and a sign of ingratitude to the man. Thus, I request you to allow me to begin at the beginning and go on till I come to the end.

Widening Access to University Education for Primary School Teachers

Senteza-Kajubi narrates how he became the Director of the NIE in several publications (e.g. Nakyondwa, 2007; Senteza-Kajubi, 2004). In Senteza-Kajubi (2004, pp. 8-9) he narrates that:

> The Castle Commission of Education in Uganda... recommended that an Institute of Education be established to provide, among other things, facilities for the study of Education in Uganda and a professional centre for teachers and the training of teachers. A search was made for... Director... and... I answered that call and in late 1964, I was appointed Director of the National Institute of Education.

The first task of the NIE, according to Senteza-Kajubi (2004), was to respond to the challenge of taking university education nearer to teachers of all grades[20] and to bring as many of them as possible to the university, which then was the one and only one, Makerere University. Ssekamwa (2008) confirms this when he asserts that:

> Senteza-Kajubi's directorship [of NIE] brought in an innovation which gave hope to teachers who had qualified as Grade II and Grade III to teach in primary schools to enrol for promotional courses which helped them to enrol for undergraduate courses at universities. This gave hope to primary school teachers that once they had ability and ambition, they could study and get undergraduate degrees, Master's… and PhD degrees. Many such former primary school teachers upgraded themselves to PhD level and some of them are now professors in universities while others hold international jobs…. (pp. 6 – 7).

---

20 There are six levels in Uganda's structure of education: 1) a non-compulsory pre-primary level; 2) seven years of primary education; 3) four years of the lower secondary (Ordinary-Level [O-Level]—leading to the Uganda Certificate of Education [UCE] award); followed by 2 years of Advanced secondary (A-Level—leading to the Uganda Advanced Certificate of Education [UACE]); 5) tertiary (which awards post-secondary diplomas); and 6) university (which awards degrees). The Ministry of Education certifies teachers at three levels: Grade III (from Primary Teachers Training Colleges, which admit holders of the UCE and award them certificates in education equivalent to the UACE); Grade V (from National Teachers Colleges [NTCs], which admit holders of the UACE and award them diplomas in education that are sequentially higher than the UACE); and Graduate (who hold degree level qualification in education). A fourth level, Grade II, used to be part of the system but has since been phased out. Hitherto, Grade II, Grade III and Grade V teachers could not access degree level education because Makerere University, the only degree awarding institution in the country, admitted only A-Level leavers on the basis of their UCE and UACE.

Widening Access to University Education for Secondary School Teachers

Senteza-Kajubi (2004) observes that the NIE "was the mustard seed out of which grew the Institute of Teacher Education Kyambogo (ITEK), now Kyambogo University which has enabled many more teachers to rise to much greater professional heights" (p. 10). It was thus right and fitting that when ITEK was established in 1986, he was appointed as its principal. Mulindwa (1998, p. 146) observes that "it was... a blessing for Kyambogo to have such a reputed scholar in the very field of education as its leader". It is also worth noting that while it had existed with several different names and locations right from 1948, it was Professor Senteza-Kajubi who succeeded in winning the "long struggle to achieve legal status for Kyambogo" (Mulindwa, 1998, p. 146), with the passing, at Senteza-Kajubi's constant nagging, in August 1989 of the Institute of Education Act, 1987, making Kyambogo autonomous for the first time (Mulindwa, 1998, p. 140).

Thus Senteza-Kajubi succeeded in making ITEK "the centre... for teacher training and co-ordination in the country... what Kyambogo had... been set up to be" (Mulindwa, 1998, p. 141). To show the significance of this achievement, Mulindwa noted that the "Statute was perhaps the best thing that has happened to Kyambogo from its inception" (p. 146). While at ITEK, Senteza-Kajubi put in place arrangements for Grade V teachers to get Bachelor of Education (BEd) degrees, moreover in only two years (Mulindwa, 1998, p. 143; Nakyondwa, 2007), and not the usual three.

Calling for the Massification of Access to Public Universities

Between 1987 and 1989, Senteza-Kajubi chaired the EPRC which advocated the widening of access to public university education through the Diploma and Mature Age Entry Schemes. At the time, Makerere University, the only degree awarding institution in the country, mainly admitted A-Level leavers holding the Uganda Advanced Certificate of Education (UACE). In contrast, the Diploma Entry and Mature Age Entry Schemes would enable more people to gain admission to the university. The commission supported the Mature Age Entry Scheme arguing that "it gives a chance to those who could not enter... university just after UACE for reasons beyond their control, and... provides opportunities to those who are late developers" (EPRC, 1989, p. 78). In addition to the Mature Age Entry Scheme, the commission advocated for the Diploma Entry Scheme, contending that "when this [Diploma Entry] system is denied to candidates with Diploma qualifications... it becomes absurd... since they are more qualified than those having UACE" (p. 78). Thus, the EPRC recommended that "candidates with national diplomas should be considered for entry to universities provided that the degree courses which they have applied for are directly related to their diploma programmes..." (EPRC, 1989, p. 78).

The EPRC also advised that such diploma entrants, "should be exempted from studying some... courses for the degrees they have been registered for" (pp. 78-79); meaning that "those exempted may complete their studies in a shorter period...." (p. 79). The EPRC recommended that "admission to... tertiary... institutions should be made available to as many qualified candidates as the physical, manpower and financial resources of institutions permit" (EPRC, 1989, p. 79). While one may argue that the EPRC was a collective voice and not Senteza-Kajubi's individual voice, his being its Chair notwithstanding, Senteza-Kajubi did several times individually debate in favour of democratisation and massification of access to public universities (see e.g. Senteza-Kajubi, 1997; 1999; 2001; 2006). For example, he consistently attacked the very Makerere University system that trained him and in which he taught and which he headed twice as being too elitist. He contended that "the original, and... inherited mission of Makerere, was that of providing a select and small class of Africans — an elite to assist the Colonial Government... to perpetuate the British culture in the Region" (Senteza-Kajubi, 1997, p. 25).

He attacked the elitist education system as intended to separate the graduates from the rest of society, thus:

> This elitism meant separating the cream... from the rest of society, through a system of free higher education which aimed at co-opting the best students as defined by the existing elite to the aristocracy of culture, which by nature had to be kept small. (Senteza-Kajubi, 1999, p. 8)

He then went ahead (e.g. in Senteza-Kajubi, 1997) to call for the massification of the access to university education by opening the gates to the public universities for all, irrespective of gender, region and family background, philosophising that "a system of higher education paid for by all, but enjoyed by a few cannot be socially and politically sustainable" (p. 25).

He further argued that "in education... the more people who participate, the better it is. Quantity enhances quality and does not diminish it" (p. 23). Senteza-Kajubi (1997) continued to stress that

> while the pursuit of excellence and the production of an elite are a proper role of universities, higher education should be accessible to as many people as possible through many different paths of access and at any rate, in many forms, especially with a view to meeting needs of individuals for continued self-improvement and development. (pp. 23–24)

Senteza-Kajubi (1997, pp. 27–28) further challenged the validity of Ordinary (O) and Advanced (A) Level criteria for admission to university education, arguing that:

> the ideal student is not necessarily the one with the highest 'A' level results, but rather the one with a passion for knowledge and determination to use the time at… university to prepare… for community service. The 'O' and 'A' level criteria that are used for admission to… universities are not adequate enough to predict suitability for university education and they leave out many individuals who would be successful university students.

Calling for the Opening of Private Universities

The EPRC advocated the liberalisation of university education by allowing the private sector to open universities. In particular, the commission endorsed the "involvement of parents, communities, voluntary agencies and other organizations of the private sector in the opening, running and financing of [higher] educational institutions" (EPRC, 1989, p. 110). In addition to the recommendations of the EPRC, Senteza-Kajubi advocated the privatisation of university education in several of his works (e.g. Senteza-Kajubi, 1997; 1999; 2001). For example, Senteza-Kajubi (1997) argued that the "liberalization and the promotion of private enterprise and initiatives in all socio-economic sectors, including education, is one way of stimulating popular participation in the development process" (p. 24).

Senteza-Kajubi (1999) contended that the "private universities... are potentially the most important avenue of widening access to higher learning without significantly increasing the financial burden to Government" (pp. 16–17). Senteza-Kajubi (1997) called for the establishment of more and more private universities to relieve the pressure on Makerere University, thus:

> Makerere has for a long time had a monopoly of university education. The new universities... being opened will help not only to relieve pressure on Makerere to expand enrolments, but may also in time lead to a more differentiated system of higher education in which each institution has its own personality and special role to play in human development. (p. 26)

Grooming Nkumba University to Maturity

In addition to advocating the widening of access to university education through the privatisation of university education, Senteza-Kajubi went ahead to lead by example, by heading one of the new private universities to maturity. In 1995, he put aside the pride of having headed Makerere University, Uganda's flagship HEI, and accepted to be the Vice Chancellor of a nascent Nkumba University. He told Nakyondwa (2007) that at the time he started heading it, the university had only 60 degree students, but he steered it until it got a charter[21] in 2007.

---

21 A charter is a legal document issued to a private university by the President of Uganda, on recommendation of the Minister in charge of Higher Education, as evidence that the university meets the requirements and standards of academic excellence set by the NCHE (Republic of Uganda, 2001). Granted on the basis of recommendations arising out of rigorous evaluation of universities' performance on attributes of quality in higher education—by a multidisciplinary panel of international experts—it is the highest indication of institutional accreditation in Uganda and it affirms Government's endorsement of the work and future of the recipient universities.

In accepting to be the Vice Chancellor of Nkumba University, Senteza-Kajubi accepted to carry several burdens, expressed in Senteza-Kajubi (1997) and Senteza-Kajubi (1999). These burdens resulted from the fact that Nkumba University was not only young but also private and lacked enough facilities due to weak financial and human resource bases. Moreover, the burdens were exacerbated by hostility from those who saw private universities as either unnecessary or unviable. Senteza-Kajubi (1997) summarised those challenges as follows:

> At the beginning all private universities have to struggle against indifference, and even hostility to get themselves established, and to survive. The difficult economy and political conditions, whereby private students find it difficult to raise money for fees, the association of public universities with high quality education and better opportunities of access to public sector employment, and the inertial colonial tradition of free tuition, accommodation and meals for all university students, all militate against the idea of private universities (p. 27).

However, Senteza-Kajubi downplayed these problems and constantly comforted those who harboured doubts about Nkumba and similar universities that such problems were neither insurmountable nor peculiar to Africa and private universities. He pointed out that:

> In the United States for example, private universities like Harvard, Yale, Princeton and the like, were the first to be established, and public (state) universities had also to struggle hard against indifference and...hostility to get themselves established, and...to survive. (Kajubi, 1997, p. 27)

Senteza-Kajubi would cite examples of now time-honoured universities that equally started humbly. For example, he recounted how "the University of North Carolina in USA in its early days had a twenty four year old President (Vice Chancellor) and a staff of three, consisting of a French ex-monk, a deserter from the British Navy and a strolling player" (Senteza-Kajubi, 1997, p. 27; 1999, p. 9).

But according to Senteza-Kajubi (1999) "with time public universities in America came of age" (p. 9), and he had no doubt, and he always openly shared this fact, that the same would one day happen to the private universities in Uganda. He would cite the Luganda proverb, *"N'ezikookolima gaali magi* (loosely translated as 'even proud cocks that now crow were once eggs') (Senteza-Kajubi, 1997, p. 27). Sometimes, he cited the Bible thus: "Despise not the day of small beginnings" (Zechariah 4: 10 in Senteza-Kajubi, 2001). And true to his prediction, Uganda Christian University received its charter in May 2004, followed by Uganda Martyrs University in May 2005 and Nkumba University in February 2007.

At the 10th graduation ceremony of Nkumba University on April 21, 2007, when the university officially received its charter, Professor Senteza-Kajubi sang the *Nunc Dimittis* (Song of Simeon) and revealed that he had always promised Professor A. B. K. Kasozi, then the Executive Director of the NCHE, that the day Nkumba University received its charter, he would sing the song to him and retire.[22] Accordingly, in February 2008, Senteza-Kajubi

---

22 According to the Wikipedia online Encyclopaedia, "Simeon was a devout Jew who had been promised by the Holy Ghost that he would not die until he had seen the Saviour. When Mary and Joseph brought the baby Jesus to the Temple in Jerusalem...Simeon was there, and he took Jesus into his arms and uttered... Now, Lord, you let your servant go in peace: your word has been fulfilled. My own eyes have seen the salvation which you have prepared in the sight of every people; a light to reveal you to the nations and the glory of your people Israel." In singing the Nunc Dimittis, Senteza-Kajubi metaphorically underlines his exceptional commitment to developing Nkumba University to maturity.

(then aged 81) retired from Nkumba University. At that time, the university's enrolment had expanded from the initial 60 to over 4,000 students (an expansion of 6,566%) and the university had grown from obscurity to prominence.

It is worth noting that while several universities in Uganda now offer weekend programmes, this avenue for access to university education started at Nkumba University in 1999 during Senteza-Kajubi's tenure. While I facilitated on the MBA programme at the University, Dr Kiwanuka-Kimbugwe and Mr Agabus Mwesigwa, respectively District Veterinary and Production Officers in Rakai District[23], requested me for an opportunity to take the programme following a weekend schedule. I led them to the Dean of the School of Business Administration, who in turn took the matter to the University Senate. In Senate, some members argued against the weekend programme, contending that teaching at weekends would deny staff and students a chance to worship on Saturdays (for the Seventh Day Adventists) and Sundays (for the other Christians). However, Senteza-Kajubi countered by reminding them of the story in the Bible wondering whether "if your sheep fell in a ditch on Sabbath, you would not retrieve it just because it is Sabbath" (Matt 12: 11–12). He equated the widening of access to university education through the weekend programme to retrieving the many who fell in the "ditch" of missing university education due to the restrictions inherent in the traditional full-time modes of university education delivery. He won the argument and the weekend programme now enrols over a third of the students in the university. Similar programmes have been introduced by most of the other universities in the country.

---

23 Rakai District is located 204 kilometres away from Nkumba University. On average, this is a four-hour journey and with the erratic road transport system in the area at the time, prospective MBA students working so far away from the university could not commute daily to attend classes on the weekday schedule.

Discussion and Recommendations

The foregoing sections demonstrate that the things Senteza-Kajubi did to expand and diversify access to university education in Uganda as well as the challenges he surmounted to do these things characterise him as a "change agent" and "champion" in the sense that authors such as Rogers (2003) and Stuart, et al. (2009) describe as explained at the beginning of this chapter. As a "change agent", he bore the vision to transform the country's university education system from an elitist to a mass one while as a "champion", he charismatically and resiliently promoted this vision of change through his leadership and effective communication — winning over pessimists and sceptics. Accordingly, Government, private universities and public universities should respectively consider the following recommendations arising out of Senteza-Kajubi's works.

Government
In view of the great contribution which the private universities can make to the national development through widening access to, and diversifying the curricular offerings in university education, Government should begin to consider private universities as part and parcel of its national human resource development strategies by giving them assistance in such forms as tax exemption and direct financial assistance (Senteza-Kajubi, 1997, pp. 17, 28).

Private universities
Private universities in their curricular offerings, teaching methods, research and admission policies, should not merely follow the trodden path by trying to catch up with public universities. Rather, they should be more innovative, go where there is no path, as it were, and leave trails of their own (Senteza-Kajubi, 1999, p. 17). In particular, private universities should be free and more innovative

to experiment with more flexible admission requirements than public universities. They could, for example, institute preliminary or remedial courses aimed at creating students out of those that are otherwise regarded as failures (Senteza-Kajubi, 1999, p. 16).

Public universities

Public universities should open their main gates as wide as possible, and have several other entrances, so as to let in as many aspirants as possible who thirst and hunger for knowledge, to have a chance to improve themselves. Let the public universities accept the young and/or private universities as comrades in arms, recalling that maybe at one time, the former were at the stage where the latter are, now. That way, what is true among American universities, as Professor Senteza-Kajubi used to say, where "there is enough space for Harvard and Howard", will happen in Uganda, where there will then be enough space for time-honoured public universities and the rather young upcoming ones. "There should be room for Ivy League type of universities as well as junior community colleges type of institutions; room for Oxbridge as well as Oxford College and Rapid Results College in London" (Senteza-Kajubi, 2005, p. 4). Let the public universities acknowledge the fact that the young and/or private universities relieve them of the pressure to increase enrolments. Eventually, "private and publicly supported universities…will stand shoulder to shoulder together to face the momentous task of transforming our higher education from an elitist to a mass tertiary education system" (Senteza-Kajubi, 1997, p. 29)

Chapter 4

Deregulation of Higher Education in Nigeria: A Call for Restraint

A. O. K. Noah, Adesoji A. Oni & Stephen D. Bolaji

Introduction

Deregulation is a process by which governments remove selected regulations on business in order to encourage operation of the market forces of demand and supply (Wokocha, 2005). It aims at providing a level playing field for businesses, which promotes competitiveness, productivity, efficiency, consumer choice and utility at the most affordable prices. The assumption underlying deregulation is that the simpler the regulation in an industry, the greater the level of participation in the industry. Drucker and Hodge (2000) support deregulation, arguing that government is good at making decisions but less so at implementing them, meaning that government should make public policies while the private sector implements these policies. Deregulation has often been pivotal to the efficiency and effectiveness of the business enterprises in the developed countries, especially in the area of basic utilities such as energy, transportation, health and education.

However, deregulation is not devoid of criticism. Sharon (2003) argues that deregulation has affected reliability in the provision of electricity in some countries due to wildly volatile wholesale prices. Crandall (2004) also notes that there exists a great concern about the concentration of media ownership resulting from the relaxation of historic controls on media ownership that were designed to safeguard diversity of viewpoint and open discussion in the society. Black (2005) also attributes gross incidence of corruption in US companies to gaps in regulation. Although eminent scholars on the subject refute these criticisms, deregulation has had substantial economic effects and engendered substantial controversy.

Deregulation in Nigeria

In Nigeria, the democratisation process ushered in 1999 ignited economic revitalisation through increased involvement of the private sector in the provision of essential services. A policy of deregulation was introduced to promote the revamping of public enterprises — known for gross inefficiency, operational losses, low return on investment and draining public funds. The deregulation experience in Nigeria is assumed to be similar in policy and scope to what is obtainable in the developed world. The goal is to provide a conducive environment for financial players to grow and contribute to the development of the nation. According to Wokocha (2005), the advocates of deregulation in Nigeria premise their position on the dysfunctional and dismal performance of public institutions and enterprises. Although, there were opposing views, opponents of deregulation failed to explain alternative ways out of the problems associated with public enterprises. Accordingly, sectors such as aviation, financial services, agriculture and, more recently, energy were deregulated. The policy of deregulation is also notable in the area of education. The springing up of HEIs founded by religious organisations, business people and philanthropists attests to this fact. The intent of this chapter is to discuss the aftermath of the deregulation policy in education within the purview of higher education, bearing in mind the sociological and philosophical implications of the policy.

Deregulation of University Education in Nigeria

Deregulation of education refers to the breaking of government's monopoly in the provision and management of education by allowing private sector actors to participate in the provision and management of education. It involves relaxation or dismantling of the legal and governmental restrictions on the operations of education. Caldwell and Spinks (1992) argue that the deregulation of education would help schools to become self-managing. In contrast, Olatunbosun (2005) analogises the deregulation of education as a sale of knowledge to the highest bidder, which may have the effect of lowering standards. As a deregulated sector, education may become a private enterprise undertaken by individuals or corporate bodies that hope to maximise profit from their investment.

In Nigeria, deregulation of university education is a recent phenomenon, born out of the realisation that private (primary and secondary) schools are better managed than public ones. Today, there are 32 private universities in the country. The deregulation of education is premised on the need for access to educational opportunities by all Nigerians, in line with the objective of building a just and egalitarian society enshrined in the National Policy on Education. Prior to the deregulation policy in 1999, less than 25% of qualified Nigerians seeking admission into universities could be offered access due to lack capacity.

Access, in this context, has different meanings and applications. The term universal access refers to the ability of all people to have equal opportunity to have a commodity regardless of social class, ethnicity, ancestry or physical disabilities. This definition is particularly well-suited to the provision of education as a service. The African Union Commission (AUC) and its International Centre for Girls and Women's Education in Africa (CIEFFA) note that in education, access goes beyond mere enrolment, progression and successful completion. It includes five dimensions: economic; physical; sociological; physiological; and cultural (CIEFFA/AUC, 2009). According to Lewin (2007), access has little meaning unless it results into more equitable opportunities to learn for students from poorer households, students with disabilities and students from under-represented ethnic backgrounds.

In Nigeria, many of these dimensions of access to university education were elusive before deregulation of the higher education sector. Today, however, there are more than eighty private institutions of higher learning complementing public institutions to achieve a common goal of making tertiary education accessible to the citizenry. However, according to Akpotu and Akpochafo (2009), increase in private HEIs is not peculiar to Nigeria. It is a global trend that is notable even in socialist leaning countries such as Tanzania, Trinidad and Tobago, Mongolia and various parts of the former Soviet Union.

Problems Associated with Deregulation of Higher Education

Deregulation of higher education in Nigeria has both sociological and philosophical implications. The policy has widened the gulf of social stratification and inequality in the country. Consumption of social goods, of which education is one, is the most visible consequence of class. Only parents who can afford to pay the increased tuition fees can send their children to school. The

Weberian concept of social stratification makes it clear that private institutions in any society create classes of distinction among the citizenry. Bourdieu (2001) also argues that class distinction and preferences are most marked in the ordinary choices of everyday existence, especially under the scope of the educational system. According to Goodson (2000), inequality in educational opportunity often deprives people of the quality of life to which all should have access. Thus, the challenge of unequal access to education as a result of economic disfranchisement remains a serious issue to be dealt with in the deregulation of education in Nigeria. This is not to be attributed to the government alone. Many members of religious organisations that have founded universities cannot afford to send their children to the universities because they cannot afford the associated costs. This is a problem in that exclusion of a large number of young people from the higher education system constitutes an imminent threat to the stability of the country's already volatile political landscape (USAID/ FGN, 2009).

From a philosophical point of view, the pragmatic nature of private HEIs is another issue. In the more developed societies, private institutions are established based on the understanding of filling a gap in a specialised area of knowledge that the public institutions may not venture into, probably as a result of lack of budgetary allocation or dearth of expertise. However, in Nigeria, there is a considerable degree of inconsistency and disharmony in objectives, curriculum and educational processes of private institutions because the majority of the institutions have no distinct area of knowledge different from the public institutions. For instance, some universities of technology offer courses in liberal arts. There is a problem when politicians, bureaucrats and the media seize upon privatisation as the main formula for developmental action. The university educational system has been in serious trouble over the last couple of years – with an unstable academic calendar, strikes in agitation for funding and other issues — yet privatisation is the main solution that has been suggested.

Deregulation, especially in a nation that has not yet fully imbibed the ethos of democracy and recognised education as a public utility, may result into a poorly educated society. Human beings are not equally endowed intellectually and economically but each person should be accorded respect and given equal opportunity to realise themselves within the limits of their intellectual capabilities (Bolaji, 2011). There are principles guiding both the educational practices and classical political democracy, which are generally regarded as the cornerstone of democracy and education. Kneeler (1971, p.23) enumerates these principles thus:

- Since the people elect their government, they should be educated to live responsibly.
- Through education, every individual is expected to develop their own talents to the full.
- Men and women must be educated to be free.
- Education should train the open mind.
- Education should develop the habit of productive cooperation as well as healthy competition.
- Whenever possible, we should adopt democratic practices in school behaviour.
- Political control over education must be kept to the minimum.

Ruwa (2007) asserts that these are necessary principles for Nigeria, whose desire is to build a strong economic and educated society.

These principles can be pursued to their logical conclusion in a disciplined and democratic country. Dewey (1916, p.89) opined that educational attainment is a prerequisite for a democratic society. He stressed that education promotes democracy and development, and because it leads to greater prosperity, it is also thought to cause political development. Buttressing Dewey's position is modernisation theory popularised by Lipset (1959); Gardner (1961, p.34); and Giroux (2003). Modernisation theory emphasises the role of education and economic growth in promoting political development in general and democracy in particular. Lipset (1959) argues that education broadens people's outlook; enables them to understand the norms of tolerance; restrains them from adhering to extremist doctrines; and increases their capacity to make rational electoral choices. However, this may not be achieved in a deregulated economy that does not see education as a public utility.

Conclusion and Way Forward

Deregulation has had positive and negative outcomes for Nigeria. However, the concern is to ensure that education is made accessible to all people irrespective of their social status. The need for educational loans for individuals to be able to achieve their educational aspirations is imperative. In a deregulated higher education setting, the cost of university education is one of the major causes of disenfranchisement from education. In a country such as Nigeria that is dogged by various forms of inequality, this presents as an important problem, since education is an important platform that promotes social transformation. Its potential to promote the development of the country's higher education sector notwithstanding, deregulation should be approached with restraint – cognisant of the risk of exclusion that it presents.

Chapter 5

Do Universities in Uganda Satisfy their International Students?

Jude Ssempebwa, Fawz N. Mulumba & Ritah N. Edopu

Introduction

Traditionally, the vast majority of students studying abroad have moved from developed to developed countries (i.e. North to North) and from less developed to more developed countries (i.e. South to North) (cf. Altbach & Knight, 2007; Altbach, 2006; Brooks & Waters, 2009a; UNESCO Institute of Statistics, 2013). An implicit assumption in both these student flows is that, in general, the students go to universities that guarantee a satisfactory level of quality in the more developed countries (see, e.g., Altbach & Knight, 2007; Brooks & Waters, 2009a; Nicolescu, 2005). However, over the last two decades, HEIs in the South have received an increasingly significant number of international students from both the South and the North (Altbach, 2006; Brooks & Waters, 2009b; Ssempebwa, Eduan & Mulumba, 2012; Teferra & Knight, 2008).

Unlike the case with the traditional (North-North and South-North) student flows, however, quality assurance in the

South-South and North-South student flows should not be taken for granted — considering that many of the HEIs in the South have been reported to be operating under encumbering funding and political constraints that could threaten quality (see, e.g., Diouf & Mamdani, 1994; Ishengoma, 2003; Mamdani, 2007; Materu, 2007; Sawyerr, 2004; Teferra & Altbach, 2003; Teferra & Altbach, 2004; Teferra & Knight, 2008). There is a need to understand whether the international students at these HEIs are satisfied with the quality of the institutions' service delivery — to ascertain the merit of this new flow and/or highlight areas requiring improvement, if any. However, review of related literature leads to the conclusion that this information is generally non-existent — apparently because scholarship on flows of students to HEIs in the South is only budding. This study was conducted to contribute to the filling of this knowledge gap, taking the case of international students at four universities in Uganda — one of the top international student receiving countries in Eastern Africa (Ssempebwa, Eduan & Mulumba, 2012).

In conducting the study, perceived quality was taken as a proxy for satisfaction. Therefore, we reviewed literature related to the meaning and measurement of quality in higher education (i.e. Bamiro, 2012; Borden & Owens, 2001; Finch, 1995; Gilroy et al, 1999; Goodlad, 1995; Green, 1995; Materu, 2007; Middlehurst & Campbell, 2003; Monash University, 2001; Salmi, 2009a; UNESCO, 2005; 1998) — to identify parameters within whose framework to examine students' satisfaction with the quality of their institutions' service delivery. The review led to two pertinent conclusions:
- Depending on its goal, measurement of quality in a HEI could be done by students, alumni, employers,

accreditation agencies and/or professional organisations who/which may collect/supply qualitative and/or quantitative data about the institutions' performance on specified standards.

- In measuring quality, focus should be put on the extent to which HEIs in a given community maintain specified standards.

The standards used in measuring quality should touch on students (i.e. qualifications, experience and motivations); faculty (i.e. qualifications, research, community service and teaching); institutional governance, academic freedom and autonomy; funding; facilities and support services; and reputation.

Judgment of institutions' performance on these standards should be contextualised, since the presence or lack of quality may be relative to context.

In Uganda, the UOTIA (2001) mandates the country's NCHE to promulgate standards of quality assurance in higher education service delivery and enforce them (Republic of Uganda, 2001). Pursuant to this mandate, the council enforces a checklist of HEI quality assurance standards. The standards touch on attributes of institutions' location, infrastructure, facilities, governance, staffing, funding, gender sensitivity, research and graduates' transition into the labour-market and the council accredits institutions whose performance on the standards is rated as "Ideal", "Good", "Acceptable" or "Improvable" (NCHE, 2004). In addition, the council periodically surveys the state of higher education delivery in the country (see, e.g., NCHE, 2006; 2010). In 2006, it also surveyed graduates of the HEIs and their employers – to generate feedback on the graduates' labour market performance (NCHE, 2006b). National and regional professional bodies (e.g. East

African Medical and Dental Council and Uganda Law Society) also evaluate and accredit study programmes. Organisations such as the Association of Commonwealth Universities (ACU) also evaluate and provide feedback on quality assurance in HEIs in the country.

However, a gap in the aforementioned efforts to evaluate quality in higher education service delivery in the country pertains to the fact that information has been sought only from alumni, employers, accreditation agencies and professional organisations. Students have been left out despite the fact that: 1) they are the ones receiving the services of HEIs; 2) some accreditation agencies do not confirm that HEIs deliver the levels of quality that the standards they maintain promise; and 3) in some instances, the agencies have expressed scepticism about quality assurance in institutions/ programmes that they accredited (see, e.g., Ahimbisibwe, 2012). Regarding international students, review of related literature (e.g. Businge & Karugaba, 2012; Inter-University Council for East Africa, 2009; Kasenene, 2009; Ouma et al., 2012) shows that quality information on the extent to which they are satisfied with the quality of service delivery in their HEIs is generally non-existent. Indeed, literature related to the reform agenda in the country's higher education system (e.g. Court, 1999; Kasozi, 2003; Mayanja, 2007; Nakanyike and Nansozi, 2003; Planning and Development Department [PDD], 2008, 2008) shows that efforts to improve quality assurance in the system have been aimed at improving quality assurance generally rather than informed by feedback from this category of students, yet international students have been reported to have peculiar expectations and challenges (Altbach & Knight, 2007; Bartram, 2007; Knight, 2007; Ouma et al., 2012). Therefore, this study delved into the extent to which international students in the country are satisfied with the quality of their receiving HEIs' service delivery.

Methodology

Conceptualisation of the study accepted, as a frame of analysis, the view from the literature that judgment of institutions' performance on attributes of quality assurance should be tied to context. Therefore, examination of the extent to which international students in Ugandan HEIs are satisfied with the quality of their institutions' service delivery was hinged on the attributes of quality assurance specified by the country's NCHE. However, effort was made not to re-invent the evaluations of the quality of higher education service delivery conducted by the NCHE and professional accreditation agencies. Focus was put only on attributes of services that HEIs are obliged to provide to the students and about whose satisfactoriness students could validly express opinions. These included teaching and library, ICT, recreation and health services. International students were asked to specify whether they found attributes of these services "Very Satisfactory", "Satisfactory", "Unsatisfactory" or "Very Unsatisfactory".

Twelve (12) attributes of the quality of teaching were identified from the literature (e.g. Bamiro, 2012; Goe, 2007; Hanushek et al., 2005; Mamdani, 2007; Wenglinsky, 2000). These were: lecturers' mastery of subject matter, encouragement of learners' participation in learning, enhancement of comprehension of course content, sensitivity to individual differences among learners, pedagogical creativity, utilisation of learners' pre-course competencies, relation of theory to practice and professionalism; conduciveness of teaching environments and utilisation of teaching aids; and evaluation of learning. Library services were looked at in terms of the size and ergonomic comfort of libraries; conduciveness of opening hours and service quality; quality of e-resources; and the quantity, relevance and currency of resources (cf. Krishna, 1996). Regarding ICT, focus was put on the ergonomic comfort of ICT labs; availability of computers; ICT accessibility and utilisation policies; and the quality of hardware, software, user support and Internet connectivity (cf. CoSN, 2001, 2003; Bakia, 2002; Trucano, 2005). Recreation services were looked at in terms of the quality of sports facilities and opportunities for involvement in sports that the universities availed to the students. Finally, the quality of health services was examined in terms of the HIEs' health policies as well as first aid and evacuation services because the institutions are obliged to ensure availability of the three irrespective of whether they run full-scale medical services or not.

Using a questionnaire, data was collected from 775 international students. These were drawn from Kampala International University, Kampala University, Kyambogo University and Makerere University, which enrolled 8,974 (representing 75%) of the 11,992 international students in the country (Table 5.1).

Table 5.1: Population and Sample

University	Location	Population of International Students[1]		Total	Sample[2]
		Male	Female		
Kampala International University*	Kampala	4853	1862	6715	364
Makerere University*,[3]	Kampala	1058	771	1829	317
Bugema University	Luwero	240	622	862	-
Busoga University	Iganga	389	372	761	-

		(Continued)			
Islamic University in Uganda	Mbale	333	154	487	-
Kampala University*	Kampala	204	196	400	196
Nkumba University	Wakiso	249	134	383	-
Uganda Martyrs University	Mpigi	91	70	161	-
Uganda Christian University	Mukono	73	70	143	-
Uganda Pentecostal University	Kabarole	51	38	89	-
Kumi University	Kumi	0	39	39	-
Ndejje University	Luwero	28	9	37	-
Kyambogo University*	Kampala	17	13	30	28
Nile University	Arua	22	6	28	-
Mbarara University	Mbarara	12	7	19	-
Gulu University	Gulu	2	2	4	-
Kabale University	Kabale	0	3	3	-
Mountains of the Moon University	Kabarole	1	1	2	-
Total		**7623**	**4369**	**11992**	**905**

[1]Culled from NCHE (2006); [2]Based on Krejcie and Morgan (1970); [3]Includes Makerere University Business School; *Included in sample of universities

The distribution of the 775 students who returned completed questionnaires is shown in Table 5.2.

Table 5.2: Distribution of Respondents

Variable	Categories	Count	Percentage
Gender	Female	324	42
	Male	451	58
	Total	775	100
Sending country	Burundi	81	10
	Kenya	328	42
	Nigeria	51	7
	Rwanda	62	8
	Somalia	134	17
	Sudan	77	10
	Tanzania	42	5
	Total	775	100
Proprietorship of university attended	Private	526	68
	Public	249	32
	Total	**775**	**100**

Findings

To gain insight into the extent to which the universities' quality of teaching, library, ICT, recreation and health services satisfy the international students, the latter were asked to specify whether they found attributes of these services "Very Satisfactory", "Satisfactory", "Unsatisfactory" or "Very unsatisfactory".

The students rated nine (9) of the twelve attributes of the quality of teaching as satisfactory. This suggests that the students were happy with the quality of teaching. However, none of the attributes was rated as being very satisfactory. The inference here is that, although the students are not necessarily dissatisfied with the quality of teaching they are given, there is still room for improving it. Moreover, only the respondents from public universities were positive about all the attributes of teaching quality investigated. The respondents from private universities rated their lecturers' professionalism, utilisation of teaching aids and feedback from evaluation of their learning as being unsatisfactory.

The respondents rated the size, ergonomic comfort and opening hours of their universities' libraries as being satisfactory. They were also positive about the service quality and currency of resources in the libraries. However, they rated the quantity and relevance of the resources as being unsatisfactory. Even on these items, the mean scores of the respondents from public universities were better than those of the respondents from private universities, except those on opening hours and service quality.

In the public universities, the students were positive about all the attributes of ICT service delivery except availability of computers. However, in the private universities, the students rated four of the seven attributes of ICT service delivery as being unsatisfactory. These included availability of computers, ICT services accessibility policies, software and Internet services. Although the respondents were positive about the ergonomic comfort of the universities' ICT labs and quality of computer hardware and ICT support, these findings suggest that this (quality) hardware was neither abundantly available to the students nor complemented by requisite software and connectivity to the Internet. This casts doubt on the quality of the universities' ICT services.

Recreation services were well rated in both the private and public universities. However, comparative examination of the findings shows that: 1) the students from public universities were more satisfied with their universities' recreation services than their counterparts from private universities; and 2) in both the private and public universities, the respondents were happier with the opportunities for involvement in sports activities their universities availed than they were with the sports facilities that the universities provided.

Regarding health services, the students from private universities indicated that they were not satisfied with the universities' health services. However, they rated the universities' ambulance services as being satisfactory. On the other hand, the students from the public universities indicated that they were satisfied with the attributes of the universities' health services except ambulance services.

Discussion and Recommendations

Our findings show that overall, the students were satisfied with most of the attributes of higher education service delivery investigated. These findings seem to account for Uganda's success in attracting a notable number of international students from the East African region and other parts of the world (cf. NCHE, 2006; 2010; Ouma et al., 2012). The findings also seem to endorse as worthwhile the flow of international students to HEIs in the country.

However, the students were satisfied with the attributes of higher education service delivery to varying degrees. In general, the students in public universities were more satisfied with the quality of higher education service delivery than their counterparts in private universities. As well, the students were more satisfied with the quality of teaching, recreation and health services than with the quality of library and ICT services. Both these findings rhyme well with those of Kasenene (2009) who found that universities in Uganda are at significantly different levels of service quality adding that while some are promising to fully become centres of excellence in higher education service delivery, others are still far below their students' expectations, particularly in terms of providing the information services that the students need to do research, enrich their knowledge and develop.

Although the country has been quite successful in attracting international students, therefore, its ability to retain these students and to attract more of them in an internationally competitive environment requires improvement of the quality of service delivery in its HEIs. Our findings suggest that this improvement is especially required in the private universities and in the areas of library and ICT services. Two observations from related literature support this suggestion. First, private universities enrol majority of the international students in the country (cf. NCHE, 2006; 2010), meaning that their ability to satisfy the students' expectations is pivotal to the country's long-term ability to attract the students. Secondly, ICT is an essential tool in the development of higher education (Bisaso, 2006; Loing, 2005; Zhao, 2003), the inference being that in international higher education provision, institutions that have unsatisfactory ICT services are likely to lag behind their competitors.

Beyond the four universities studied in Uganda, the fact that the gaps in the HEIs' service quality the international students cited were mainly in private HEIs and in the areas of library and ICT services is particularly relevant to the study of the flow of international students to HEIs in the South. Authors such as

Altbach (2006; 2005) and Kasozi (2003) express scepticism that a big number of the privately owned HEIs mushrooming in various countries in the South have emerged as mere demand-absorbing diploma mills established to make quick profit for their owners rather than to deliver higher education services of a satisfactory level of quality. As well, a host of authors (e.g. Mamdani, 2007; Oyebade & Keshinro, 2007; etcetera) observe that gigantic enrolment expansion — under the auspices of the neoliberal structural adjustment reforms implemented in most countries in the South over the last three decades — resulted in a situation where HEIs enrol more students than their resources can accommodate at satisfactory levels of quality. Regarding ICT services, studies such as Bakia (2002) and Ssempebwa, Bakkabulindi and Sekabembe (2012) concluded that many HEIs in the South do not meet the total cost of owning satisfactorily functional ICT services. These authors suggest that the things international students in Uganda were found to be less satisfied with are endemic in HEIs in the South. The inference here is that although our study vindicates — as giving a satisfactory experience — the flow of international students to HEIs in the South, sustaining and encouraging this flow may require that attention is paid to the quality of service delivery in the privately-owned HEIs in the region and to the satisfactoriness of library and ICT services.

Chapter 6

Attributes of Human Capital Developed by Ugandan Universities and Students' Post-Graduation Motives

Livingstone Ddungu

Introduction

Human capital refers to the stock of knowledge and innate and acquired attributes that embody the ability that underlies a person's productivity (Døving & Nordhaug, 2002). The level at which the human capital developed by a university meets students' post-graduation motives gives some indication of the degree to which the university equips students with the knowledge and skills that they need to achieve their motives and contribute to the development of their society (Chan, Brown & Ludlow, 2014; Schwartz, 2003). The higher this level is perceived to be, the higher the university's level of effectiveness is perceived to be and vice-versa (Massy, 2011; Byrne & Flood, 2005). Therefore, ensuring high levels of convergence between universities' teaching and their students' post-graduation motives is a vital strategic goal that any university wishing to win a competitive edge in the global higher education market should not ignore (Liu, 2010; Mazzarol & Soutar, 2002).

Unfortunately, in Uganda, the level at which universities realise this goal has been questioned. For instance, many of the universities' graduates are not as productive as society expects them to be (Nabayego, 2011; Ministry of Education, 2003). They neither get nor create jobs (Mwesigwa, 2014; Lule, 2013; Action Aid International Uganda et al., 2012; World Bank, 2008; Nabulya, 2013; Mwesigwa, 2014; Ntambaazi, 2013). It is against this background that this study has attempted to respond to the following questions: 1) What attributes of human capital do universities in Uganda develop in their students? 2) What are the post-graduation motives of the students in these universities? 3) What is the relationship between the attributes of human capital universities in Uganda develop in their students and the students' post-graduation motives?

Related Literature and Knowledge Gap

Concept of Human Capital

Nurturing the human capital needed to address the development needs of society has been the subject of extensive scholarship (see, e.g., Radwan & Pellegrini, 2010; Dae-Bong, 2009; Djeflat, 2009; Amidon, Piero & Mercier-Laurent, 2005; Døving & Nordhaug, 2002; Xiao, 2001; Becker, 1964; Schultz, 1981). In their typology of labour economics, Schultz (1981) and Becker (1964) postulate different perspectives of the human capital theory to explain the fact that capital does not include only the money needed to facilitate acquisition of other factors of production. It also includes human capital. Becker's (1964) perspective of this theory defines human capital as any stock of knowledge or characteristics innately possessed or acquired by an individual and which contributes to his or her productivity. It is also defined as an amalgam of factors such as education, experience, training, intelligence, energy, work habits, trustworthiness, and initiative that contributes to a person's productivity (Djeflat, 2009). Human capital is further regarded as the expandable, shareable and marketable labour force, which includes intellectual property and other talents (Dae-Bong, 2009). This is derived from Schultz's (1981) perspective of the human capital theory, which posits that the purpose of any investment in education or training should be to improve the productivity of learners by developing their stock of knowledge and shaping a variety of other human capital attributes such as learners' self-awareness, self-regulation, self-motivation, social competence and positive attitudes towards work (Amidon et al., 2005).

An analytical look at the scope of human capital implied by Becker's (1964) and Schultz's (1981) perspectives and the other definitions given above reveals that human capital is very broad. It includes all the information, facts, descriptions or skills gained cognitively and emotionally through perception, communication, association, reasoning or discovery based on experience or education (Gottschalk-Mazouz, 2008; Cavell, 2002).

In educational institutions such as universities, this stock includes all the understanding imparted to learners theoretically and practically (Djeflat, 2009). It has an implicit dimension (which includes theoretical expertise) and an explicit dimension (competencies or visible/practical skills) (Eddy, 2013). This stock can be imparted as communicating knowledge (Winzenried, 2011; Tho, Hui, Fong & Tru Hoang, 2006). It can be inculcated as situated knowledge or as partial knowledge, since most knowledge is inculcated and acquired in parts (Bengson & Moffett, 2011; Stroud, 2011; Pritchard, 2007). It can further be imparted as scientific knowledge, that is, instilled and acquired through gathering observable and measurable evidence subject to specific principles of reasoning and experimentation (Amin, 2005). Knowledge can be general or task-specific (Cook & Mansfield, 2013). In this study, focus was put on the general and task-specific dimensions of knowledge because all the other dimensions can be categorised under these two broad dimensions.

General knowledge is also referred to as academic knowledge (Brianna & Ashleigh, 2013), general metacognition or generic skills, and is defined as information, facts, processes and principles that are broad in nature and theoretical in form (Furnham, Christopher, Garwood & Neil, 2007; Veenman & Spaans, 2005). Imparting this type of knowledge involves instilling in learners facts, concepts, assumptions, theories and principles that explain or underlie phenomena (Burson, Larrick & Klayman, 2006). Examples of general knowledge include scientific, mathematical, chemical, physical, biological, cultural, social, economic, geographical, historical, philosophical, psychological, anthropological, sociological, political, organisational, management, accounting, engineering and a variety of other concepts, principles, processes and networks that are, by nature, not specific (Døving & Nordhaug, 2002). Advocates of general knowledge argue that it promotes analytical and all-purpose reasoning and dynamic adjustment to the changing world conditions, thereby facilitating flexibility, career mobility and competitiveness (Døving & Nordhaug, 2002). These advocates further argue that by not being tied to a particular task or industry, general knowledge helps in solving a wide range of tasks.

Task-specific knowledge, also called specific metacognition or technical, professional, specialised or industry-specific knowledge, is defined as skills that a person applies to do particular tasks or to solve particular problems (Van der Stel & Veenman, 2008; Veenman, & Verheij, 2001). Learners are equipped with this knowledge using activity-based education so that they can gain knowledge, skills and competencies needed to continue doing similar activities even after graduating from the training (Nabayego, 2011). In fact, it has been observed that this type of knowledge enables students to improve their productivity, leading to improvement in their rewards (Djeflat, 2009) and contribution to societal economy (Dae-Bong, 2009). These observations suggest that when learners are exposed to activity-based education, they gain knowledge, skills, competencies and experience that students can use to engage in activities by which they may transform surrounding environmental resources into valuable commodities. Accordingly, data were collected on the extent to which the universities' teaching exposes their students to these attributes of human capital.

Students' Post-Graduation Motives

The concept of motive has two meanings, one being given by psychologists and another by sociologists. Psychologists such as Zimmerman (2000) define it as any condition or event within an organism that impels or directs behaviour toward attainment of a goal. Based on this definition, psychologists such as David McClelland, cited in Kulwinder (2011), defined a motive as an invisible, intrinsic or inner force whose visible form is manifested in terms of outcome expectations. The specific motive identified by David McClelland is the achievement motive, which he defined as a desire to meet realistic goals. For students, this includes developing mastery in doing something, acquiring the skills needed to excel in life, being competitive in the labour market, and experiencing a sense of accomplishment (Kulwinder, 2011;

Trusty, 2000). Another motive is a power motive, defined by David G. Winter, cited in Baumeister and Kathleen (2007), as the need to be influential and recognised in society or the intention to have impact, reputation, prestige, and pleasure after attaining a desired goal. For students, the power motive is expressed in terms of having a positive contribution to their families, adding value to the economy through increased productivity offering professional services that enhance the quality of life and getting a highly paying and prestigious job, among others (Byrne & Flood, 2005). Zimmerman (2000) points out that another motive that compels students in school is the need to improve self-efficacy so that they are in a position to organise and execute anticipated courses of action and attain designated goals effectively. Improving self-efficacy implies acquiring more intellectual abilities, practical knowledge as well as skills needed to do work better, more efficiently and effectively.

The sociological definition of motive was given by Max Weber, cited in Swatos (nd.), as a complex of subjective meaning which, to the actor, seems to be an adequate ground for given conduct. This suggests that a motive is an explanation given to justify involvement in a given behaviour. Contemporary sociologists such as Scott (2010) have largely accepted this definition. They justify the definition basing on the functional theory, which explains the reasons that account for behaviour. Scott (2010) also explains that motives underlie actions and may be a result of conscious and unconscious beliefs on the moral and social conditions of society. Using a sociological definition, Robert (nd.) identifies a public service motive as a common motive that people tend to have, especially those who want to work for public institutions and organisations, or who have a deeper desire to make a difference by making an impact on public affairs with a sense of responsibility and integrity. According to Mann (2013), this motive is more expressed in terms of intrinsic rewards such as a desire to engage in meaningful public service and altruism or willingness to serve in the public interest as opposed to salary or job security, promotions, and other extrinsic motives. Mwesigwa (2014) contrasts Mann's (2013) observations by arguing that students dream big, hoping that after graduation, they will work with large companies and earn a good wage. This argument supports Bagraim's (2013) observation that people's public service motives are grounded in enlightened self-interest expressed in a belief that personal motives coincide with those of the larger community. So, people's personal identification with public service programmes or organisations is rooted in self-interest. This argument is supported by the profit motive, which maintains that the intent of transactions or endeavours that involve meeting some costs is to realise some gains. This seems applicable to university students, since they (and/or their sponsors) incur costs to attain their education (Radwan & Pellegrini, 2010).

Sheppard (2013) indicates that the different motives that tend to underlie students' pursuit of education can be categorised as intrinsic, career and extrinsic. In support, Chan et al. (2014) observe that students seek to receive university education to improve their skills and get better placements in the job market. This suggests that students expect university education to prepare them in a manner that enables them to succeed in the job market. Chan et al. (2014) further add that students are also motivated by the fact that after graduation, their parents expect them to support them by educating their siblings and uplifting the quality of life of the parents' households. According to Wells (2010), one of the main post-graduation motives students hold is their desire to attain self-fulfilment. Students want to live a better life, having gainful employment and being able to meet all their short- and long-term needs, and to support their kin and society as a whole. Earlier on, Brailsford (2010) and Liu (2010) had made similar observations, categorising students' post-graduation motives into personal or intrinsic motives and extrinsic motives. Brailsford (2010) observes that personal motives include a sense of mastery and achievement and career considerations such as entry into the academia, getting a better paying job, earning a promotion, and other personal goals. Extrinsic motives include fulfilling parents or family and society expectations (Mazzarol & Soutar, 2002). Malick and Grisay (2000) observe that students' post-graduation motives include being more innovative, competently productive, developing a career, becoming employable and useful in society.

Among other things, the authors cited above show that students' post-graduation motives may be diverse and complex, touching on many things. Upon careful examination, the views that the authors express underline the need for generating quality information about these motives. This is especially true in contemporary higher education, where quality has been defined in terms of the fit between expectations and experiences. Hitherto, however, systematised inquiry into Ugandan university students' post-graduation motives had not been conducted. This study was conducted to close this gap. Specific attention was paid to the attributes of students' post-graduation motives identified by the authors on the subject cited above.

Methodology

The study was conducted following a cross-sectional survey design. Data were elicited using a structured questionnaire, from a sample of 384 students drawn from a target population of

130,198. These students were enrolled at twelve (12) universities, which were randomly selected for involvement in the study from a target population of seventeen (17). The size of the samples was determined using Krejcie and Morgan's (1970) Sample Size Estimation Table. The students involved in the study were selected using convenience sampling (based on accessibility). The content validity index (CVI) and Cronbach Alpha coefficient of the questionnaire were respectively established at .908 and .836. The data collected was analysed using percentages, means, Pearson Correlation and linear regression.

Findings and Discussion

To understand the students' perceptions of the attributes of human capital their universities develop, the students were asked to indicate the extent to which they "Agree" that the universities develop features of human capital characterised in the literature. The extent of agreement was expressed on a five-point Likert Scale thus: "Strongly Agree", "Agree", "Not Sure", "Disagree" and "Strongly Disagree". The findings were that more students "Agreed" or "Strongly Agreed" that their universities developed the attributes of general knowledge investigated (Table 6.1). However, they were not as positive regarding industry-specific knowledge. Table 6.2 shows the distribution of the students by extent of agreement that they held specified post-graduation motives.

Table 6.1: Attributes of Human Capital Developed by the Universities (%, N = 384)

Attributes	Indicators	SD	D	NS	A	SA	Total	Mean	St. D
General knowledge	My course is improving my general reasoning ability		2	8	40	50	100	4.66	.076
	My course is improving my communication skills	2	10	24	40	24	100	4.35	.035
	My course of study is enhancing my ability to explain phenomena		20	25	31	24	100	4.01	.093
	The skills my course is giving me are theoretical			22	38	41	100	4.50	.017
Task-specific knowledge	My course is giving me entrepreneurial skills	28	39	20	8	6	100	2.35	.069
	My course is giving the skills required in my industry	32	40	9	17	2	100	2.43	.015
	My course is equipping me with the skills I need to secure employment	36	28	17	10	9	100	2.24	.023
	My teachers simulate job-related experiences in their teaching	40	28	21	9	2	100	1.47	.011

Table 6.2: Students' Post-Graduation Motives

(%, N = 384)

Attributes	Indicators	SD	D	NS	A	SA	Total	Mean	St.
Intrinsic	I want to develop the intellectual abilities I need to use after university		12	6	40	42	100	4.69	.0
	I want to lay a firm foundation for my economic security	7	14	3	31	46	100	4.96	.0
	I want to improve my self-worth	6	7	2	52	33	100	4.63	.0
	I want to improve my social status	3	10	25	26	37	100	3.97	.0
Extrinsic	My parents encourage me to get a degree	0	1	18	36	45	100	4.17	.0
	My parents want me to get a degree to enhance the status of our family	2	17	11	36	34	100	4.52	.0
	My community wants me to get a degree so that I contribute to its development	3	12	26	27	31	100	4.17	.0

		SD	D	NS	A	SA	Total	Mean	St. D
	(Continued)								
Employability	I want to acquire skills that will enable me to become employable			24	34	42	100	4.67	.067
	I want to acquire skills that will enable me to become productive			15	42	43	100	4.83	.071
	I want to acquire skills that will enable me to become innovative			5	36	59	100	4.66	.018
	I know that getting a university degree will enable me to get a good job		3	12	14	71	100	4.58	.097
Career-related	I want to build an attractive CV		4	12	41	43	100	4.63	.033
	I want my training to help me to earn better		0	7	21	73	100	4.83	.016
	I want to improve my professional career	5	11	23	24	37	100	4.56	.092
	I want to earn a promotion at work			20	36	43	100	4.73	.019

KEY: SD = "Strongly Disagree"; D = "Disagree"; NS = "Not Sure"; A = "Agree"; SA = "Strongly Agree"; St. D = Standard Deviation

Table 6.2 shows that the response options "Agree" and "Strongly Agree" attracted the majority of the students on all the attributes of post-graduation motives investigated. This confirms that, as is suggested in the literature, the students' post-graduation motives relate to employability and career and that they are both intrinsic and extrinsic.

The third research question focused on analysing the relationship between the attributes of human capital that the universities develop and the students' post-graduation motives. To analyse the relationship, the students' responses to the questions on the attributes of human capital developed and those on the attributes of post-graduation motives were respectively computed into indices. The indices were then correlated using Pearson Product Moment test (Table 6.3).

Table 6.3: Relationships between Attributes of Human Capital Developed and Students' Post-Graduation Motives

			Attributes of Human Capital	
			General Knowledge	Task specific knowledge
Post-Graduation Motives	Intrinsic	Pearson Correlation	.344*	-.4*
		Sig.(2-tailed)	.00	.00
		N	384	384
	Extrinsic	Pearson Correlation	.318*	-.362*
		Sig(2-tailed)	.00	.00
		N	384	384
	Employability	Pearson Correlation	.441*	-.436*
		Sig. (2-tailed)	.00	.00
		N	384	384
	Career-related	Pearson Correlation	.449*	-.49*
		Sig. (2-tailed)	.00	.00
		N	384	384

Table 6.3 shows that significant relationships were established between all the attributes of the students' post-graduation motives and human capital. However, the relationships with attributes of task-specific knowledge were inverse. It should also be noted that for all the variables, the indices of relationship were less than 0.5, meaning that the relationships were weak. Linear regression analysis was conducted to ascertain whether these relationships were causative (Table 6.4).

Table 6.4: Prediction of Post-Graduation Motives by the Attributes of Human Capital Developed

	Error	Standardised Beta	t	Sig.	R-Square	Adjusted R-Square	F	Sig.
Constant			12.995	.000	.209	.205	65.001	.000
General knowledge	.068	.025	0.223	.381				
Task-specific knowledge	.009	-.428	-14.2	.000				

The findings in Table 6.4 suggest that the stock of knowledge imparted by the universities predicts students' post-graduation motives only by 20.5%. For 79.5% of the students, the human capital developed does not facilitate realisation of post-graduation motives. This appears to explain why many of the universities' graduates are unable to get or create jobs (Mwesigwa, 2014; Nabulya, 2013; World Bank, 2008). The universities need to increase attention to industry-specific knowledge in their training programmes. The findings presented in Table 6.4 show that most of the students "agreed" that the universities developed their human capital by imparting general knowledge. However, the corresponding mean suggests that the degree to which the universities did this was low. As well, the specific forms of knowledge that were imparted at a low level included knowledge that students needed to improve their communication ability and to broaden their understanding of the principles needed to explain phenomena within their study areas. Since communication and understanding of principles underlying phenomena are crucial in reinforcing industry/task-specific knowledge, the universities need to improve the level at which they impart these forms of knowledge in their students.

Chapter 7
The Importance of Research in a University[24]

Mahmood Mamdani

Introduction

My remarks will be more critical than congratulatory. I will focus more on the challenge we face rather than the progress we have made. My focus will also be limited, to the Humanities and the Social Sciences rather than to the Sciences, to postgraduate education and research rather than to undergraduate education.

I would like to begin with a biographical comment. I did my 'O-Levels' at Old Kampala Secondary School in 1962, the year of [Uganda's] independence. The US government gave an independence gift to the Uganda government. It included 24 scholarships. I was one among those who were airlifted to the US, getting several degrees over 10 years — BA., MA, PhD — and returned in 1972.

Those who came with me divided into two groups. There were those who never returned, and then those who did, but were soon frustrated by the fact that the conditions under which they were supposed to work were far removed from the conditions under

---

24 This is a slightly edited version of a paper delivered as a keynote address by the author at the Sixth Annual Makerere University Research Conference. Also disseminated previously as Makerere Institute of Social Research (MISR) Working Paper Number 3, the paper is published herein with the kind permission of the author.

which they were trained. In a matter of years, sometimes months, they looked for jobs overseas, or moved out of the academia into government or business or elsewhere. The lesson I draw from my experience was that the old model does not work. We have no choice but to train postgraduate students in the very institutions in which they will have to work. We have no choice but to train the next generation of African scholars at home. This means tackling the question of institutional reform alongside that of postgraduate education.

Postgraduate education, research and institution building will have to be part of a single effort. I would like to put this in the context of the history of higher education in Africa. I do not mean to suggest that there is a single African history. I speak particularly of those parts of Africa colonised after the Berlin Conference in late 19th century. There is a contrast between older colonies such as South Africa or Egypt where Britain embarked on a civilising mission — building schools and universities — and newer colonies such as Uganda where they tended to regard products of modern education as subversive of the existing order.

History of Higher Education in Africa

You can write a history of higher education in Africa that begins a millennium ago. It is now well known that there existed centres of learning in different parts of Africa — such as Al-Azhar in Egypt, Al-Zaytuna in Morocco, and Sankore in Mali — prior to Western domination of the continent. And yet, this historical fact is of marginal significance for contemporary African higher education. This is for one reason. The organisation of knowledge production in the contemporary African university is everywhere based on a disciplinary mode developed in Western universities over the 19th and 20th centuries.

The first colonial universities were few and far between: Makerere in East Africa, Ibadan and Legon in West Africa, and so on. Lord Lugard, Britain's leading colonial administrator in Africa, used to say that Britain must avoid the Indian disease in Africa. The Indian disease referred to the development of an educated middle class, a group most likely to carry the virus of nationalism.

This is why the development of higher education in Africa between the Sahara and the Limpopo was mainly a post-colonial development. To give but one example, there was one university in Nigeria with 1,000 students at independence. Three decades later, in 1991, there were 41 universities with 131,000 students. Nigeria is not an exception. Everywhere, the development of universities was a key nationalist demand. At independence, every country needed to show its flag, national anthem, national currency and national university as proof that the country had indeed become independent.

We can identify two different post-independent visions of the role of higher education. One was state-driven. I spent six years teaching at the University of Dar es Salaam in the 1970s. The downside of the Dar es Salaam experience was that governments tended to treat universities as parastatals, undermining academic freedom. The great achievement of Dar es Salaam was the creation of a historically-informed and inter-disciplinary curriculum.

A later post-independence vision was market-driven. Makerere University came to be its prime example. I spent nearly two decades at Makerere, from 1980 to 1996. During the 1990s, Makerere combined the entry of fee-paying students [privatisation] with the introduction of a market-driven curriculum [commercialisation]. The effects were contradictory: payment of fees showed that it was possible to broaden the financial base of higher education;

commercialisation opened the door to a galloping consultancy culture.

The two models had a common failing. Neither developed a graduate programme. Everyone assumed that post-graduate education would happen overseas through staff development programmes. I do not recall a single discussion on post-graduate education at either Dar es Salaam or Makerere.

A Pervasive Consultancy Culture

Today, the market-driven model is dominant at African universities. The consultancy culture it has nurtured has had negative consequences for postgraduate education and research. Consultants presume that research is all about finding answers to problems defined by a client. They think of research as finding answers, not as formulating a problem. The consultancy culture is institutionalised through short courses in research methodology, courses that teach students a set of tools to gather and process quantitative information, from which to cull answers.

Today, intellectual life at universities has been reduced to bare-bones classroom activity. Extra-curricular seminars and workshops have migrated to hotels. Workshop attendance goes with transport allowances and per diem. All this is part of a larger process, the 'NGO-isation' of the university. Academic papers have turned into corporate-style power point presentations. Academics read less and less. A chorus of buzz words have taken the place of lively debates.

If you sit in a research institution as I do, then the problem can be summed up in a single phrase: the spread of a corrosive consultancy culture. Why is the consultancy mentality such a problem? Let me give you an example from the natural sciences.

In 2007, the Bill and Melinda Gates Foundation decided to make eradicating malaria its top priority. Over the next four years, it spent US$150 million on this campaign. Even more important were the consequences of its advocacy programme, which was so successful that it ended up shaping priorities of others in the field of health. According to a recent study on the subject, WHO expenditure on eradicating malaria skyrocketed from US$100 million in 1998 to US$2 billion in 2009. The rush to a solution was at the expense of thinking through the problem from an epidemiological point of view. There are two kinds of diseases: those you can eradicate, such as sleeping sickness or smallpox, and those you cannot such as yellow fever — because it lives on a host, in this case monkeys, which means you would have to eradicate monkeys to eradicate yellow fever.

The two types of diseases call for entirely different solutions: for a disease you cannot eradicate, you must figure out how to live with it.

Last year, a team of scientists from Gabon and France found that malaria too has a wild host — monkeys — which means you cannot eradicate it. To learn to live with it calls for an entirely different solution. Eradication calls for a laboratory-based strategy. You look for isolated human communities, such as islands with small populations and invest all your resources in it — which is what the Gates Foundation and WHO did. But living with malaria requires you to spend your monies in communities with large, representative populations. The Gates Foundation and WHO money was spent mostly on small islands. A WHO expert called it 'a public health disaster'. The moral of the story is that diagnosis is more important than prescription. Research is diagnosis.

Creating an Antidote to the Consultancy Culture

How do we counter the spread of the consultancy culture? Through an intellectual environment strong enough to sustain a meaningful intellectual culture. To my knowledge, there is no model for this on the African continent today. It is something we will have to create.

The old model looked for answers outside the problem. It was utopian because it imposed externally formulated answers. A new model must look for answers within the parameters of the problem. That is why the starting point must go beyond an understanding of the problem, to identifying initiatives that seek to cope with the problem. In the rest of this talk, I will seek to give an analysis of the problem and outline one initiative that seeks to come to grips with it. This is the initiative at the Makerere Institute of Social Research.

The Consultancy Problem Let me return to my own experience, this time at MISR, where I have learnt to identify key manifestations of the consultancy culture.

I took over the directorship of MISR in June of 2010. When I got there, MISR had seven researchers, including myself. We began by meeting each for an hour: what research do you do? What research have you done since you came here? The answers were a revelation: everyone seemed to do everything, or rather anything — at one time primary education, the next primary health, then roads, then HIV/AIDS, whatever was on demand! This is when I learnt to recognise the first manifestation of consultancy: a consultant has no expertise. His or her claim is only to a way of doing things, of gathering data and writing reports. He or she is a Jack or a Jane of all, a master of none. This is the first manifestation.

Even though consultancy was the main work, there was also some research at MISR. But it was all externally-driven, the result of demands of European donor agencies that European universities doing research on Africa must partner with African universities. The result was not institutional partnerships but the incorporation of individual local researchers into an externally-driven project. It resembled more an outreach from UK or France rather than a partnership between relative equals.

Next, I suggested to my colleagues that our first priority should be to build up the library. I noticed that the size of our library had actually been reduced over the previous 10 years. I understood the reason for this when I looked at MISR's 10-year strategic plan. The plan called for purchasing around 100 books for the library over 10 years. In other words, the library was not a priority. The second manifestation of a consultancy culture is that consultants do not read, not because they cannot read, or are not interested in reading but because reading becomes a luxury, an after-work activity. Because consultancies do not require you to read anything more than field data and notes.

My colleagues and I discussed the problem of consultancy in meeting after meeting, and came up with a two-fold response. Our short-term response was to begin a programme of seminars, two a month, requiring that every person begin with a research proposal, one that surveys the literature in their field, identifies key debates and locate their query within those debates; second, also twice a month, we agreed to meet as a study group; prepare a list of key texts in the social sciences and humanities over the past 40 years, and read and discuss them.

Over the long-term, we decided to create a multi-disciplinary, coursework-based, PhD programme to train a new generation of researchers. To brainstorm the outlines of this programme, we held a two-day workshop in January with scholars from University of Western Cape in South Africa and Addis Ababa University. I would like to share with you some of the deliberations at that workshop.

Reflections on Postgraduate Education in the Humanities and the Social Sciences

The central question facing higher education in Africa today is what it means to teach the humanities and social sciences in the current historical context and, in particular, in the post-colonial African context. What does it mean to teach humanities and social sciences in a location where the dominant intellectual paradigms are products not of Africa's own experience, but of a particular Western experience? Where dominant paradigms theorise a specific Western history and are concerned, in large part, to extol the virtues of the enlightenment or to expound critiques of that same enlightenment? As a result, when these theories expand to other parts of the world, they do so mainly by submerging particular origins and specific concerns through describing these in the universal terms of scientific objectivity and neutrality?

I want to make sure I am not misunderstood: there is no problem with reading texts from the Enlightenment – in fact, it is vital. The problem is this: if the Enlightenment is said to be an exclusively European phenomenon, then the story of the Enlightenment is one that excludes Africa as it does most of the world. Can it then be the foundation on which we can build university education in Africa?

The assumption that there is a single model derived from the dominant Western experience reduces research to no more than a demonstration that societies around the world either conform to that model or deviate from it. The tendency is to de-historicise and de-contextualise discordant experiences, whether Western or non-Western. The effect is to devalue original research or intellectual production in Africa. The global market tends to relegate Africa to providing raw material ("data") to outside academics who process it and then re-export their theories back to Africa. Research proposals are increasingly descriptive accounts of data collection and the methods used to collate data. Collaboration is reduced to assistance. And there is a general impoverishment of theory and debate.

The expansion and entrenchment of intellectual paradigms that stress quantification above all has led to a peculiar intellectual dispensation in Africa today. The dominant trend is increasingly for research to be positivist and primarily quantitative, carried out to answer questions that have been formulated outside of the continent, not only in terms of location but also in terms of historical perspective. This trend either occurs directly, through the "consultancy" model, or indirectly, through research funding and other forms of intellectual disciplining. In my view, the proliferation of "short courses" on methodology that aim to teach students and academic staff quantitative methods necessary for gathering and processing empirical data are ushering a new generation of native informers. But the collection of data to answer pre-packaged questions is not a substantive form of research if it displaces the fundamental research practice of formulating the questions that are to be addressed. If that happens, then researchers will become managers whose real work is to supervise data collection.

But this challenge to autonomous scholarship is not unprecedented — indeed, autonomous scholarship was also denigrated in the early post-colonial state when universities were conceived of as providing the "manpower" necessary for national development, and original knowledge production was seen as a luxury. Even when scholars saw themselves as critical of the state, such as during the 1970s at University of Dar es Salaam, intellectual work ended up being too wedded to a political programme, even when it was critical of the state. The strength of Dar es Salaam was that it nurtured a generation of public intellectuals. Its weakness was that this generation failed to reproduce itself. This is a fate that will repeat in the future if research is not put back into teaching; and PhD programmes in Africa are not conceived of as training the next generation of African scholars.

Someone told me yesterday that Makerere requires every PhD thesis to end with a set of recommendations. If true, this indicates a problem. A university is not a think tank. A university may house think tanks, even several, but a university cannot itself be a think tank. Think tanks are policy-oriented centres where the point of research is to make recommendations. In a university, there needs to be room for both applied research, meaning policy-oriented research, and basic research. The distinction is this: unlike applied research which is preoccupied with making recommendations, the point of basic research is to identify and question assumptions that drive the very process of knowledge production.

The Postgraduate Initiative at MISR

I believe one of the biggest mistakes made in the establishment of MISR as a research institute was to detach research from postgraduate education. The formation of the new College of Humanities that has brought the Faculties of Arts and Social Sciences and MISR under a single administrative roof gives us a historic opportunity to correct this mistake. MISR will aim to offer a multi-disciplinary doctoral programme in the qualitative social sciences and the humanities.

The initiative at the Makerere Institute of Social Research (MISR) is driven by multiple convictions. One, key to research is the formulation of the problem of research. Two, the definition of the research problem should stem from a dual engagement: on the one hand, a critical engagement with the society at large and, on the other, a critical grasp of disciplinary literature, world-wide, so as to identify key debates within the literature and locate specific queries within those debates.

Faced with a context where the model is the consultant and not the independent researcher, we at MISR think the way forward is to create a PhD programme based on significant preparatory coursework, to create among students the capacity to both re-think old questions and formulate new ones. Our ambition is also to challenge the foundations of the prevailing intellectual paradigm which has turned the dominant Western experience into a model which conceives of research as no more than a demonstration that societies around the world either conform to or deviate from that model. This dominant paradigm de-historicises and de-contextualises other experiences, whether Western or non-Western. The effect is to devalue original research in Africa. Research proposals are increasingly descriptive accounts of data collection and the methods used to collate data, collaboration is reduced to assistance, and there is a general impoverishment of theory and debate. If we are to treat every experience with intellectual dignity, then we must treat it as the basis for theorisation. This means to historicise and contextualise not only phenomena and processes that we observe, but also the intellectual apparatus used to analyse these.

Finally, MISR will seek to combine a commitment to local [indeed, regional] knowledge production, rooted in relevant linguistic and disciplinary terms, with a critical and disciplined reflection on the globalisation of modern forms of knowledge and modern instruments of power. Rather than oppose the local to the global, it will seek to understand the global from the vantage point of the local. The doctoral programme will seek to understand alternative forms of aesthetic, intellectual, ethical, and political traditions, both contemporary and historical, the objective being not just to learn about these forms, but also to learn from them. Over time, we hope this project will nurture a scholarly community that is equipped to rethink — in both intellectual and institutional terms — the very nature of the university and of the function it is meant to serve locally and globally.

Coursework
Coursework during the first two years will be organised around a single set of core courses taken by all students, supplemented by electives grouped in four thematic clusters:
- Genealogies of the Political, being discursive and institutional histories of political practices;
- Disciplinary and Popular Histories, ranging from academic and professional modes of history writing to popular forms of retelling the past in local languages;
- Political Economy, global, regional and local; and

- Literary and Aesthetic Studies, consisting of fiction, the visual and performing arts and cinema studies.

Translated into a curricular perspective, the objective is for an individual student's course of study to be driven forward by debates and not by orthodoxy. This approach would give primacy to the importance of reading key texts in related disciplines. In practical terms, students would spend the first two years building a bibliography and coming to grips with the literature that constituted it. In the third year, they would write a critical essay on the bibliography, embark on their own research in the fourth year, and finally write it up in the fifth.

Inter-disciplinarity

Over the 19th century, European universities developed three different domains of knowledge production — natural sciences, humanities, and social sciences — based on the notion of "three cultures". Each of these domains was then subdivided into "disciplines." Over the century from 1850 to the Second World War, this became the dominant pattern as it got institutionalised through three different organisational forms: a) within the universities, as chairs, departments, curricula, and academic degrees for students; b) between and outside universities at the national and international level, as discipline-based associations of scholars and journals; and c) in the great libraries of the world, as the basis for classification of scholarly works.

This intellectual consensus began to break down after the 1960s, partly because of the growing overlap between disciplines and partly because of a shared problematique. For example, the line dividing the humanities from the social sciences got blurred with the increasing "historicisation" and hence "contextualisation" of knowledge in the humanities and the social sciences. The development was best captured in the report of the Gulbenkian Commission chaired by Immanuel Wallerstein. As inter-disciplinarity began to make inroads into disciplinary specialisation, the division between the humanities and the social sciences paled in the face of a growing division between quantitative and qualitative perspectives in the study of social, political and cultural life.

But these intellectual developments were not matched by comparable organisational changes, precisely because it is not easy to move strongly entrenched organisations. Although the number of interdisciplinary and regional institutes multiplied, collaboration rarely cut across the humanities-social science divide.

The challenge of postgraduate studies at the African university is how to produce a truly interdisciplinary knowledge without giving up the ground gained in the disciplines. The challenge of MISR is how to reproduce a generation of researchers by joining research to postgraduate education. Our incorporation into the new College of Humanities and Social Sciences, and thereby an end to our stand-alone status, has created this opening for us — one we hope to seize with both hands.

Chapter 8

University Governance and Intellectual Capital at two Universities in Uganda

Karim N. A. Ssesanga

Introduction

Universities in both developed and budding economies are knowledge-intensive organisations that contain basic operations for knowledge generation, sharing, and transfer. As such, their intellectual capital potential is great. However, only some of them are able to transform this potential into operational intellectual capital. In particular, African universities currently function in very difficult circumstances, both in terms of the social, economic, and political problems that afflict the continent and in the context of globalisation (Teferra & Altbach, 2004). Indeed, in the Ugandan context, universities are characterised by doing more with less (Ssesanga & Garrett, 2005).

The concept of good governance has been topical for many scholars. Research in this respect has focused on how the two impact on the profitability of corporations and businesses. However, this trend started to take root in higher education, with the growing need for an educated society and the realisation that traditional approaches of running and managing universities were inadequate (Aurangzeb & Khola, 2012). In fact, concern about governance has been heightened not only in the corporate world but also in HEIs (Akma et al., 2013).

The ability of any university to thrive hinges on its capacity to properly use all its financial, physical, and intellectual resources. In this paper, I focus attention on intellectual capital as a vital and strategic asset that denotes the valuable knowledge in an organisation (Griliches, 1990; Barrett and Beaver, 1991; Michalisin et al., 1997; Nonaka & Takeuchi, 1995; Mouritsen, 1998).

Good governance denotes the process whereby both public and private institutions guarantee human rights in the conduct of public affairs, and operate in a manner that cherishes the rule of law, and creates an environment essentially free of abuse and corruption (OECD, Year). In higher education, governance and management increasingly concern themselves with knowledge systems and workers. Thus, the utility of higher education governance and management models will be judged in terms of how well they allow the HEIs to contribute to further the knowledge society and economy (Reed et al., 2002).

Among the characteristics of a good university, therefore, is the ability to attract and retain talented academics who have the ability to contribute significantly to advances in research (Yusof, 2008). Academics are considered to be intellectual capital — the most vital resource of any university. It is vital for universities to manage these academics effectively so that they transform their potential into operational intellectual capital.

The argument in this study is premised on the hypothesis that bad governance can lead to inability to attract and retain intellectual capital. The study surveys the perceptions of faculty (at

two universities in Uganda — one public and one private) on the subject. Specifically, the study sought to achieve three objectives:
- To examine academics' perception of intellectual capital and governance practices at the two universities;
- To examine the factors that attract and retain academics at the two universities; and
- To examine the relationship between governance and intellectual capital at the two universities.

Related Literature

The word governance provokes thoughts of power or authority to make things happen (Mkude, 2012). Governance encompasses the structures, relationships and processes through which policies for higher education are developed, implemented and reviewed (OECD, 2008:68).

According to Tricker (1984:7) "management is about running the business" whereas "governance is about seeing that it is run properly". Thus, at a university, good governance sets the rules for the relationship between management and academics and the activities for generating, sharing, and disseminating knowledge. It is not enough for any organisation to acquire human capital. Increasingly, organisations are faced with the need to adopt and incorporate structures and processes that effectively deploy, protect and retain their human capital (Bontis, 1996; Bradley, 1997; Keenan & Aggestam, 2001). On their part, universities need to develop their intellectual capital and to transform it into a competitive advantage.

Intellectual capital has three main components: human, structural and relationship (Stewart, 1999; Sveiby, 2001). Human capital consists of knowledge, experience, competence, intelligence, creativity, values and attitudes. Structural capital includes management relationship, organisation structure and development. On the other hand, relationship capital refers to the marketing relationship, which includes all the resources linked to the external relations of the organisation with its customers, suppliers and/ or partners and the perceptions that they hold about the organisation.

Several researchers contend that intellectual capital has a significant importance for obtaining a competitive advantage and for the capacity of an organisation to create value (Stewart, 1999; Peltoniemi, 2006). In the past, research on knowledge management and intellectual capital focused on companies. However, lately, there is an increased interest in public organisations, including universities. This is mainly due to the fact that universities have as their main goals the production and the dissemination of knowledge (Sanchez et al., 2006).

In the light of the foregoing, university managers should facilitate the work of the researchers. In particular, faculty should be given the resources they require and governance processes should be devoid of constraining dictates of bureaucracy (Azmi, 2006). Furthermore, universities should ensure that their academics have opportunities for training and career development because career development could increase job satisfaction and increase chances for attracting and retaining talented faculty (Bontis & Serenko, 1997).

Equally important, university top management should match rewards to performance in a bid to attract and retain intellectual capital as academics may find it a worthless experience to give more to an organisation when not much is received in return. This has implications on the way the university is governed.

Methodology

Data were collected using a questionnaire whose questions were adapted from Akma et al. (2013). The adaptation was done in a way that facilitated comparison of the views members of faculty in the public and private universities held about university governance and human capital. The questionnaire was divided into five parts and a five-point Likert scale (from strongly disagree to strongly agree) was used for each question. Part 1 examined the importance of intellectual capital to the university. Part 2 requested faculty to mention the factors they considered vital when joining their universities. It also requested them to give their views on the association between governance and the attraction and retention of intellectual capital. Part 3 elicited the respondents' perceptions of the governance practices in their universities — with regard to transparency, integrity, corruption, policies and procedures. Part 4 captured other aspects of governance (i.e. intellectual capital management and support for research and innovation and their impact on faculty performance). Finally, Part 5 sought the demographic composition of the respondents.

Data were collected from two universities: one public (University A) and the other private (University B). The two were selected based on their size. To avoid bias, academics from the two universities were selected randomly. Table 8.1 shows the distribution of the population and sample of respondents.

Table 8.1: Population and Sample

Variable	Categories	University A Sample (N=98)	University B Sample (N=57)
Gender	Male	76	41
	Female	22	16
Age	Below 25 years old	2	-
	26-30 years old	41	32
	31-35 years old	19	12
	36-40 years old	13	6
	41-45 years old	7	4
	46-50 years old	14	1
	Above 50 years old	2	2
Academic rank	Assistant Lecturer	9	16
	Lecturer	74	38
	Senior Lecturer	12	2
	Associate Professor	2	1
	Professor	1	-
Level of education	Professional Degree	-	-
	Bachelor Degree	14	16
	Masters Degree	77	39
	Doctoral Degree	7	2

Data were analysed using frequency counts, percentages, means and standard deviation. At the bivariate level, analysis involved the use of Pearson's correlation matrix to establish the relationship between governance and intellectual capital. Pearson's matrix was selected because the variables were numerical.

Findings and Discussion

The findings on the respondents' perception of the importance of intellectual capital in their universities are summarised in Table 8.2.

Table 8.2: Perception of the Importance of Intellectual Capital

	University A			University B		
	N	Mean	Standard Deviation	N	Mean	Standard Deviation
University's success depends on input of academics	98	4.4	.822	57	4.37	.858
University's reputation and progress depend on its academics	98	4.32	.832	57	4.16	1.031
University recognises that its academics attract new ones	98	4.3	.802	57	4.12	.965
University's competitiveness improves with increase in its intellectual capital	98	4.22	.880	57	3.98	.876

The results in Table 8.2 show that the 98 responding academics in university A agreed that the success of the university depends on the contribution from academics with the highest mean value of 4.4, followed by the notion that the university's reputation and improvement rely on its academics (mean value of 4.32). These findings are consistent with Yusof (2008)'s assertion that intellectual capital is the leading resource for universities. The findings also seem to concur with the notion that the university's reputation hinges mainly on the input of faculty. Indeed, in Uganda, as elsewhere, the quality of a good tertiary institution is determined by the quality and dedication of the academic staff (Kasozi, 2009; Ssesanga, 2003).

Furthermore, the results show that respondents at university A agree that existing academics attract new ones, and the competitive position of the university improves with the increase of its intellectual capital (mean value of 4.3 and 4.22, respectively). Therefore, responding academics at University A (which is public) agree that the quality and calibre of existing scholars was a key factor and consideration in attracting new academics to the university. The findings are congruent with Assem et al. (2008) who reported that new academics were attracted to a university by the quality of existing scholars.

At university B, the respondents agreed that the success of their university depends on the input of academics, and that competitiveness of the university improves with the increase of its intellectual capital with mean values of 4.61 and 4.4, respectively.

The results suggest that at both public and private universities in Uganda, academics agree that their input is critical for the success of the universities and that the competiveness of the universities improves with increase of their intellectual capital. This further corroborates the findings of Yusof (2008) and Kasozi (2009) in Malaysia and Uganda, respectively.

The study also focused on the factors that the academics considered vital in joining a university (Table 8.3).

Table 8.3: Factors Considered in Joining University

	University A			University B		
	N	Mean	Standard Deviation	N	Mean	Standard Deviation
I joined university because it pays better	98	4.61	.755	57	4.46	.927
Governance is a key factor in attracting new academics to a university	98	4.40	.714	57	4.33	1.139
I joined university because of its location	98	4.40	1.072	57	4.21	.959
I joined university because of its reputation	98	4.23	.950	57	4.19	.875

(Continued)						
I joined this university because I believe it will add value to my academic advancement	98	4.15	.923	57	4.09	.987

The most important factor academics considered in joining university A was pay (mean of 4.61). Governance and location of the university were the second and third considered factors, respectively (mean score of 4.4). Reputation of the university, and the belief that the university will add value to academics' reputation were considered the least important factors with mean values of 4.23 and 4.15, respectively. At university B, responding faculty considered pay and location of the university as the most important factors that influenced their decision to join university with mean values of 4.46 and 4.33, respectively. Academics at university B considered governance and the belief that the university will add value to their academic advancement as the least important factors rated at mean values of 4.19 and 4.09, respectively. While responding academics at university A considered pay and governance as the leading factors that influenced their decision to join the university, faculty at university B agreed that pay and location are the most important factors. Considering that the physical structure of most of universities in Uganda is limited to few buildings (Kasozi, 2009), and given that most private universities in Uganda are located in rural or semi-urban areas where attractions of urban areas are visibly absent, it would seem sensible to argue that faculty, particularly in private universities in Uganda, perceived location as a critical factor that influenced them to join university. As opposed to mean levels at university A, the relatively low means of 4.21 and 4.09 on reputation of the university, and the belief that university will add value to faculty academic advancement, respectively, at university B seem to concur with the assertion that all private universities in Uganda were established after 1988, and thus, lack a history and the prestige attached to past achievements (Kasozi, 2009).

Therefore, the evidence in Table 8.3 suggests that pay is the most important factor that academics consider in joining both public and private universities. This supports Ssesanga's (2003) finding that pay is a leading predictor of academic job dissatisfaction in Uganda. Additionally, governance and location are the second and third most important factors that influence academics' decisions in joining a university in Uganda. The findings are inconsistent with Akma et al. (2013) who found pay to be the least likely factor to influence academics' decisions to join university in Malaysia. This could be attributed to the fact that in Malaysia, being a tiger economy, pay for academics is much higher compared to their counterparts in a developing country such as Uganda. It appears, therefore, that in under-resourced and budding universities in the least developed countries such as Uganda, pay is an important factor to academics, especially considering that they operate under adverse and declining circumstances (Senteza-Kajubi, 1992; Saint, 1992). Besides, most of the institutions of higher learning in Uganda are running on deficit budgets (Kasozi, 2009).

The third aspect of the analysis considered the respondents' perceptions of governance and intellectual capital management at university A (Table 8.4).

Table 8.4: Perception of University Governance Practices

	University A			University B		
	N	Mean	Standard Deviation	N	Mean	Standard Deviation
There are guidelines to clarify the responsibility of all academics	98	4.06	.883	57	4.46	.927
University is a well governed institution	98	4.05	1.161	57	4.25	.931
Our work supports the mission and vision of university	98	3.98	1.339	57	4.07	.979
There is a potential for corruption at the university	98	3.87	1.281	57	4.05	1.007
University emphasises inter-organisational relationships	98	3.82	1.125	57	4.05	.915
University's policies and procedures are clearly defined for all academics	98	3.09	1.465	57	4.02	.876
My rights at university are well protected	98	3.07	1.115	57	3.88	1.070
University emphasises collaboration among colleagues	98	3.01	1.214	57	3.81	.934
University is a transparent organisation	98	2.96	1.166	57	3.79	1.013
University has a proper system for dissemination of information	98	2.90	1.351	57	3.70	1.117
University's policies and procedures are the same for all academics	98	2.81	1.265	57	3.67	1.354
Accurate and relevant information in university is easy to access	98	2.70	1.105	57	3.21	1.423
Academics are encouraged to give suggestions on how to improve the operations within University	98	2.54	1.415	57	3.16	1.251

(Continued)						
University takes the necessary corrective action in case of wrongful behaviour committed by its academics	98	2.37	1.319	57	2.70	1.669
Academics are encouraged to take part in the decision making process	98	2.06	1.346	57	2.23	1.268

Table 8.4 shows that a big number of academics agree that there are guidelines that spell out their responsibilities, and that the university is a well governed institution – rated at a mean of 4.06 and 4.05, respectively. Additionally, many respondents rated at a mean of 3.98 perceived that their work supports the mission and vision of university, and that the university emphasises collaboration at a mean of 3.82. This suggests that the university council has among others, identified and focused on the key competencies and specialisation of the university.

Nonetheless, there are areas of concern with respect to good governance practices in the university that merit scholarly attention. In particular, although responding academics agree that overall, the institution is well governed, and their rights are well protected at a mean of 3.07, it is worrying to note that a good many respondents at a mean of 3.87 believed that there is potential for corruption at the university. This finding concurs with Kasozi (2009) who maintains that many institutional leaders in Uganda are unwilling to reveal income and expenditure statements, and firmly believe that the financial records of their universities are a confidential matter. Thus, based on this evidence, it is plausible to opine that there is a potential for corruption at some universities in Uganda. This may explain why only few respondents agreed that the university was a transparent organisation, and encouraged them to take part in decision making at low means of 2.96 and 2.06, respectively, as shown in Table 8.4. Equally important, it can be seen in Table 8.4 that there were very few respondents who agree that university policies and procedures are the same for all academics (Mean of 2.81), and accurate and relevant information in university is easy to access (mean of 2.71). This suggests that, as perceived by respondents, there was unfair treatment to faculty at the university, and restricted access to information at the university which echoes the need to improve governance practices at the university.

Regarding respondents' perceptions of governance and management of IC at university B, the data in Table 8.4 reveals that very many respondents agreed that the university emphasises inter-organisational relationships, and collaboration among colleagues, at a mean of 4.46 and 4.25, respectively. The findings could be explained by the fact that private universities in Uganda put emphasis on, and engage in, collaboration because most of them have partners abroad who facilitate them with human and material resources.

Therefore, while many respondents at university A agree that the university is a well governed institution with clear guidelines and where their work supports the mission and vision of the university, at university B, very many respondents perceived that the university has policies and procedures that are clearly defined to faculty, and much emphasis was put on inter-organisational and interpersonal collaboration. Partly, I attribute this to the low staffing levels at private universities in Uganda where there is a likelihood for academics to understand policies and procedures easily, as opposed to fairly large numbers of academics and bureaucratic tendencies at public universities.

Furthermore, it is important to note that very few responding academics (a mean of 2.70) at university B agree that the university was a well governed institution, and comparatively few agree that it was transparent (mean of 3.21). These data emerging from the survey would seem to suggest that institutional heads at private universities in Uganda, unlike their counterparts at public universities, tend to wield more influence in decision making and policy direction.

It can be seen in Table 8.5 that very many respondents at university A (with a mean of over 4) agree on all the four items, indicating that there were still barriers to access corporate information.

Table 8.5: Perception of Transparency and Disclosure

	University A			University B		
	N	Mean	Standard Deviation	N	Mean	Standard Deviation
University should be more transparent in evaluation system	98	4.61	.755	57	3.81	.933
University should be more transparent in financial allocation	98	4.21	.959	57	3.79	1.011
University should be more transparent in imposing new rulings	98	4.05	.883	57	3.67	1.124
University should be more transparent in provision for facilities	98	4.04	.882	57	3.21	1.423

In particular, respondents agree that the university should be more transparent in evaluation system, and financial allocation as well as provision for facilities. The findings are congruent with the plight of most African universities particularly in the sub-Saharan region. For instance, the rapid expansion of public university education in Kenya in the midst of limited financial resources has led to deterioration of public universities in areas such as the quality of teaching and research, library facilities, halls of residence and student and staff representation (Amutabi, 2002; Oketch, 2004); and Kenyan public universities have lost their former glory due to low motivation of students and staff and poor infrastructure (Ogom, 2007). However, the data collected from university B shows a slightly different picture. The respondents (with a mean of less than 4.00) in the private university agree that they have a better evaluation system, and more transparent in financial allocation as well as provision for facilities as opposed to faculty at the public university. This finding could be attributed to the less bureaucracy, and relatively small size of private universities in Uganda in terms infrastructure. In fact, some of the new private universities in Uganda have one or two building structures with low staffing levels (Kasozi, 2009).

With regard to the efficiency of intellectual capital management at university A, Table 8.6 shows that many respondents strongly agree that if their work is appreciated, their performance improves, and everybody takes credit for their work with mean values of 4.74 and 4.53, respectively.

Table 8.6: Perception of Intellectual Capital Management

	University A (N = 98)		University B (N = 57)	
	Mean	Standard Deviation	Mean	Standard Deviation
If my work is appreciated, my performance improves	4.74	.647	4.65	.767
At university, everyone takes credit for his/her own work	4.53	.763	4.35	.954
University has a fair reward system	3.63	1.380	3.49	1.428
University encourages my research work	3.57	1.276	3.35	1.541
University has the necessary tools to evaluate my competency	2.86	1.464	2.77	1.376
University management system facilitates the work of academics	2.73	1.404	2.72	1.373
My intellectual (knowledge, skills and competencies) contributions improved at university	2.69	1.380	2.56	1.464
University encourages creativity and innovation	2.55	1.168	2.44	1.376
University rewards new ideas and outstanding output	2.23	1.267	2.39	1.485
I am motivated to do research because other faculty members do	2.01	1.366	2.37	1.345
University provides the necessary resources to achieve my research work	1.97	1.231	1.86	1.260

The results are insightful to university leaders in Uganda notably to appreciate the work of academics as this would improve their performance. This finding is consistent with available evidence among academics in Uganda to the effect that the level of faculty motivation has a significant effect on their productivity (Bameka, 1996; Ssesanga & Garrett, 2005). Furthermore, leaders at university A should maintain the spirit of ensuring that everyone takes credit for their work.

Nonetheless, there are areas of concern that merit attention and deserve improvement. In particular, in terms of research, university A should improve in areas such as encouraging faculty creativity and innovation (mean of 2.55), reward of new ideas and outstanding output (mean of 2.23), and provision of necessary resources to academics to do research work (mean of 1.97). These data are not surprising. Globally, since the 1990s, academics throughout the world have faced a number of problems, changes and status transformations (Altbach, 2002; Askling 2001, Shattock, 2004; Shattock, 2004; Honan & Teferra, 2001; Enders, 2001). They have suffered reductions in income, deterioration of working conditions and prestige (Altbach, 2002). Precisely, participating universities, like others in Uganda, are teaching-intensive institutions where teaching is the primary activity (Ssesanga & Garrett, 2005). Besides, most lecturers at universities in Uganda just manage to cover their teaching responsibilities and do not have the time or resources to do research and produce knowledge (Kasozi, 2009).

Academics at university B agree that their intellectual potential improved at the university suggesting that they find their stay at the institution a skills- and competency-enriching experience. I attribute these data to the fact that academics in most private universities in Uganda are relatively new in the profession and seem to be excited about their new experience. Furthermore, there are areas of convergence with regard to the academics' perception of intellectual management at university A and university B that should be sustained and improved.

Table 8.6 shows that the academics at both institutions agree that if their work is appreciated, their performance improves. Furthermore, both institutions encourage the research work of their faculty, as well as everyone taking credit for their own work. In addition, academics at both universities agree that more should be done to encourage creativity and innovation, facilitate the work of academics, and provision of necessary resources for faculty to achieve their research work. Indeed, academics in Uganda are dissatisfied with facilities and funds for research (Tizikara, 1998; Ssesanga & Garrett, 2005). These data have insightful information for leaders at both universities with regard to research support, to which I will turn in the recommendations.

Pearson's Correlation coefficient for the relationship between governance and (attraction and retention) of intellectual capital is shown in Table 8.7.

Table 8.7: Relationship between Governance and Intellectual Capital

		Governance	**Intellectual Capital**
Governance	Pearson Correlation	1	.86**
	Sig. (2-tailed)		.00
	N	155	155

**. Correlation is significant at the 0.01 level (2-tailed).

Table 8.7 shows that the higher the respondents rated the governance of their universities, the higher the intellectual capital that the universities would attract and retain ($r = .86$). These findings render support to studies done elsewhere (i.e. Assem et al., 2007; Nor & Akma, 2012; Akma et al., 2013).

Conclusions and Recommendations

This study leads to the conclusion that although good governance is a vital predictor of faculty attraction and retention, the key factors that attract faculty to the participating universities were pay and the prospect of academic development. In addition, the analysis reveals that whereas the private universities need to improve on their academic staff's opportunities for academic growth, pay and job security, public universities should focus on improving transparency, pay and communication. Therefore, it is recommended that universities improve their performance in these areas through improving their governance practices as discussed in the foregoing section.

Chapter 9

Prospective Graduates' Perception of the Responsiveness of Ethiopian Universities to Contemporary Labour Market Needs

Demewoz Admasu Gebru

Introduction

Higher education in Ethiopia spans over 1,700 years. However, establishment of the country's modern higher education system started in 1950. Growing rather slowly until the mid-1990s, the sector has expanded sporadically over the last two decades, moving from elite to mass. From two universities during the early 1990s, the sector has expanded to 35 public universities and over 70 private universities in 2014. Universities are being established in all parts of the country – based on considerations for regional equity.

Some of the universities were formed by merging colleges or faculties (e.g. Bahr Dar University). Others were established by state legislation (e.g. Wello University); while others only evolved progressively (e.g., Haramya University). However, they are all governed, financed and supervised by the Federal Government. All degree programmes are crafted and supervised by the Federal Ministry of Education. Hence, all public universities in the country are meant to serve the same missions – teaching, research, and community service. Starting in 2009, states were also allowed to establish regional universities (Federal Democratic Republic of Ethiopia [FDRE], 2009). Following the expansion, undergraduate enrolment rose from 203,399 in 2006/7 to 494,103 in 2011/12. However, it remains to be seen whether the phenomenal expansion of prototype programmes, guidance and counselling will produce competent graduates who are employable.

In this knowledge economy, public universities in Ethiopia are instrumental to national development. They are expected, among other things, to produce quality and competent graduates befitting the labour market. Hence, they need to be responsive to the needs of both the graduates and the labour market. With the re-introduction of the market economy in Ethiopia in 1991, demand for an educated workforce has grown (Tjeldvoll, Welle-Strand & Bento, 2005). However, the labour market has not been able to absorb the graduates of these universities because the economy remains primarily agrarian. Accordingly, students need proper vocational guidance and counselling — teaching and learning that aims at equipping students with the knowledge and skills that the labour market envisages; and research that influences policy and practice.

Given their long established tradition of autonomy, universities worldwide decide on issues such as their enrolment, teaching and research. However, following recent developments, universities are accountable to public authorities as well. These authorities require universities to provide quality and relevant education that leads to employment of graduates and to supply the labour market with competent and employable graduates. As argued by Teferra (2011), university training and education need to be aligned with the existing job market. This is critically important to Ethiopia today. For one, public spending in the sector over the last two decades is sporadically high. Second, the country is ambitiously planning and working to be middle income in the next decade. Also, Ethiopia is striving to become competitive in an increasingly globalised knowledge economy.

In line with this national imperative and global competitiveness, university leaders and staff must make adjustments in their offerings in a more responsive and innovative manner. This will allow the universities to plan and execute flexible academic programmes that align their teaching and students' learning with the demands of the contemporary labour market.

Employers need graduates who are familiar with the world of work (Barten, 2006). The process of producing this kind of graduates requires the participation of pertinent stakeholders. The participation should be in the areas such as programme initiation, curriculum development, guidance and counselling, tracer studies and policy advocacy. This is because universities whose academic programmes and teaching capitalise on students' potential and interest, and which conduct tracer studies, are more likely to produce employable graduates. In particular, public universities ought to specify the intended outcomes of courses and to work with students in reporting upon the outcomes. Since public interest is best served by a university system that maximises the knowledge, skills and values learned by university graduates (Dill, 2001), there is a need to measure programme effectiveness — to demonstrate whether the programme met its purpose and whether it needs to be adjusted.

Government, the private sector and students create employment opportunities. Universities need to address multifaceted objectives such as the quality, relevance and efficiency (Salim, 2007) of their programmes. These include knowledge of subject matter, methodological skills, ability to learn as jobs change and the professional competence of graduates. From a student perspective, a major purpose of public universities is to develop competencies that lead to gainful employment. From an employer perspective, graduates must have transferable knowledge, skills and attitudes that enable them to work individually and collaboratively (Nunan, 1999; Baren, 2006). However, producing competent graduates that are relevant to the demands of the labour market is not only a matter of training programmes; it also requires a strategy for career education, information and guidance.

Universities need up-to-date data on recruitment criteria (Barten, 2006), to design strategies for the labour market and to predict future trends. However, in developing countries such as Ethiopia, where employment data is scarce and graduate unemployment is high, universities are often accused of offering programmes of poor quality that have little relevance to the labour market (Salmi, 2009b). It is against this background that this study delved into prospective graduates' perceptions of the responsiveness of Ethiopian public universities to contemporary labour market needs. Because prospective graduates are on the verge of completing their university training, knowing their perception of how well they are prepared and how competently they could join the labour market would be useful. In addition, their lived experience, and discussions with peers would allow them to identify strengths and gaps, if any.

The study attempted to respond to three specific research questions: 1) how do prospective graduates in Ethiopia perceive the fit between the focus of their study programmes and contemporary labour market needs? 2) How do prospective graduates in Ethiopia perceive the suitability of the teaching and learning processes they are going through for the demands of the contemporary labour market? 3) To what extent would prospective graduates in Ethiopia agree that their institutions provide the vocational guidance and counselling they require to succeed in the contemporary labour market?

Methodology

Three universities were involved in the study. These were purposely selected to represent the three generations in Ethiopia's universities as identified by Gebru (2014). A sample of 250 prospective graduates was selected for involvement in the study. These were aged between 20 and 27 (mean=21). The majority (86%) of the respondents were male. The selection of the participants considered field of study (i.e. vocational, professional and academic streams) and area of specialisation (i.e. science/ technology and arts/ humanities).

Data were collected using a questionnaire. The first section of the questionnaire elicited the respondents' bio data. The questionnaire also contained questions on the focus of academic programmes (8 items); focus of teaching and learning processes (9 items); and the vocational guidance and counselling services provided to students (6 items). These items elicited the level of agreement through rating from 1 to 5. There was also one item where participants were expected to identify the body responsible for graduate unemployment. The open-ended item intended to solicit opinion of participants on the overall graduate preparation and related services provided to them. A five-point Likert scale questionnaire ranging from "1", corresponding to "Strongly Disagree" to "5", corresponding to "Strongly Agree", was used to tap into the respondents' perceptions on the attributes investigated. The validity of the questionnaire was ascertained by three experts, who provided feedback on the suitability of the items included.

Data collection took place between January and April 2012. The principal researcher, together with three onsite research assistants collected the data. Two-hundred and fifty (250) questionnaires were dispatched for self-administration. One hundred and ninety (190) (representing 76%) of the questionnaires distributed were retrieved. The data collected were analysed using frequency counts and percentages. The responses to the open-ended item in the questionnaire were subjected to content analysis.

Findings and Interpretation

The findings are summarised in Table 9.1.

Table 9.1: Level of Agreement that Higher Education Addresses Attributes of Relevance to the Labour Market
(N=190, %)

Attribute		SA	AG	UD	DA	SD	Total
Focus of academic programmes	My study programme focuses on technological advancement	41	27	12	10	11	100
	My study programme provides theoretical understanding of my field of study	46	36	10	4	5	100
	My study programme focuses on practical application of knowledge	31	28	13	13	15	100
	The courses in my study programme are valued in the labour market	18	25	28	14	15	100
	My study programme is in line with the labour market policies of the country	18	25	28	14	15	100
	My study programme addresses relevant global market needs	16	29	26	13	17	100
	My study programme provides a good mix between academic and professional education	16	26	26	13	21	100
	My field of study matches the needs in the contemporary labour market	25	27	18	15	15	100

		(Continued)					
Suitability of teaching & learning processes for contemporary labour market	The courses in my programme are innovated to suit the needs of the labour market	29	29	18	10	13	100
	The textbooks used for my programme are suited to the needs of the labour market	24	28	19	15	14	100
	My instructors frequently change the course content they deliver	17	28	19	18	18	100
	My instructors frequently change the teaching methods they use	19	26	24	16	15	100
	My instructors frequently change the assessment methods they use	22	31	20	16	11	100
	My instructors focus on skills that enhance employability	25	29	15	14	17	100
Vocational guidance & counselling	My instructors provide guidance on the opportunities available in the labour market	19	27	25	16	12	100
	My instructors provide guidance on the challenges in the contemporary labour market	25	29	15	14	17	100
	My instructors provide information on national employment strategies	20	25	13	18	24	100
	My instructors provide information on international employment strategies	13	26	20	19	22	100
	My instructors provide information on the skills I need to compete in the labour market	14	18	26	20	22	100
	My instructors guide me to choose fields of study that are congruent with my aptitude	7	20	19	22	31	100

KEY: SD = "Strongly Disagree"; D = "Disagree"; UD = "Undecided"; A = "Agree"; SA = "Strongly Agree"; St. D = Standard Deviation

The results in Table 9.1 show that the respondents perceived the public universities to be emphasising "theoretical understanding of field of study" (46 + 36 = 82 agreed). Theoretical understanding believed to be highly emphasised, technological advancement, practical application of knowledge, and the mix between field of study and professional education follow respectively. Most of the respondents believed that global market needs, labour market value of courses, match between field of study and labour market needs and labour market policy of the country are emphasised. On the other hand, about a third were "undecided"; while close to a quarter disagreed over the emphasis given to the mix between academic and professional education. Similarly, over a quarter disagreed on the emphasis of academic programmes to practical application of knowledge, labour market value of each course, labour market policy of the country, and global market trends. Over a fifth disagreed on the emphasis of academic programmes to technological advancement. As such, the findings in Table 9.1 suggest that academic programme development in the selected universities does not put strong emphasis on the demands of the labour market (e.g. technological advancement). Consequently, the graduates of these universities may feel that their academic programmes do not enable them to qualify for jobs or to create their own employment opportunities.

Regarding the focus of teaching and learning processes, Table 9.1 shows that emphasis was reported to be on theoretical understanding, practical application of knowledge, skills that enhance employability of graduates, changing traditional teaching methods and technological advancement. About a third of the respondents believed that less emphasis was put on the suitability of textbooks, innovativeness of courses of study, changes in traditional course content and skills that enhance graduates' employability. Meanwhile, over a quarter of the respondents indicated that their instructors do not change their teaching and assessment methods in line with technological advancement. Similarly, close to a quarter of the respondents suggested that practical application of knowledge is not emphasised.

These findings reveal that teaching and assessment in the case universities remain traditional, despite very significant changes in the knowledge economy and in the competitiveness of the contemporary labour market. Viewed from a constructivist perspective of assessment for learning, and from the point of view of technological advancement and innovation, this seems to go contrary to the needs of the (national and international) graduate labour market. Related literature suggests that this labour market requires the opposite to what was reported to be the case in the case universities. It demands graduates who have knowledge about modern technology, and are innovative, life-long learners and versatile.

Concerning vocational guidance and counselling, the findings in Table 9.1 suggest that the students are not getting appropriate vocational guidance and counselling services. With exception of "employment opportunities", the majority of the respondents "disagreed" that their universities provide vocational guidance and counselling-related services. This finding is despite the fact that students who are not placed in fields of study based on potential and preference are not likely to excel. The inference here is that, from entry to exit, students should be aware of their potential, available employment opportunities and the skills they need to qualify for these opportunities. On the contrary, the findings of this study suggest that this is not the case in Ethiopia, which appears to account for the escalating incidence of unemployment among university graduates in the country.

In responding to the open-ended question (pertaining to the incidence of graduate unemployment and to who takes primary responsibility for the problem), the majority of the respondents felt that there are more graduates seeking employment opportunities than the labour market is able to accommodate. They blamed this mismatch on government. Nevertheless, listening to stakeholders in the process of developing, implementing, evaluating and reviewing academic programmes would benefit the university education system as a whole. Therefore, universities should elicit the participation of pertinent stakeholders in their curriculum development processes.

Proper vocational guidance and counselling includes a strong institutional arrangement that works towards enhancing the employability of graduates through studying relevant labour market trends; proving students with the information they require about the labour market; and supplying information about the labour market to inform curriculum development. In fact, at the systemic level, it can suggest policies and strategies for addressing the incongruence between university training and labour market needs. Conversely, this was not found to be the case in Ethiopia (Table 9.1). The findings suggest that students are not well informed about the labour market (in terms of opportunities, challenges, policies and strategies). This suggests that offices established to provide vocational guidance and counselling fail to provide it. This casts doubts about the responsiveness of the universities to the demands of the labour market.

Chapter 10

Challenges of University Governance in Malawi

Lester Brian Shawa

Introduction

In this chapter, I present two arguments: first, that university governance in Malawi is being negatively affected by the global neoliberal orthodoxy — a market view of citizenship that defines a citizen as an economic maximiser who is governed by self-interest and thus views higher education as a commodity on the market that is to be competed for by those who can afford to buy it (Lynch, 2006). I argue that changes in global university governance, which follow the global neoliberal orthodoxy represent what I term "anti-democratic modes of governance". Second, that university governance is hampered by the interventionist nature of policy-steerage by the Malawi government. I contend that a combination of the two challenges poses serious threats to university governance mechanisms in the country.

Recent legal frameworks in sub-Saharan African universities generally reflect trends associated with the neoliberal orthodoxy (Saint, 2009). Put briefly, the neoliberal agenda celebrates strong market-driven policies against the central role of states in national economic development (Samoff & Carrol, 2004). It is pertinent to note, however, that while classical liberalism saw state power as negative in limiting freedoms, neoliberalism sees state power as positive in advancing market mechanisms (Olssen, Codd, & O'Neill, 2004). The latter has thus market-oriented influence on university governance supported by states.

While, on the one hand, Malawi is grappling with the demands of the global neoliberal agenda at universities, the country also suffers from the local reality of the interventionist model of policy-steerage by the government. The interventionist model is sometimes confused with state control. However, its likening to state control is problematic in that the interventionist model is "not a systematic policy control model, rather intervention occurs when higher education institutions become sites of opposition to the development path or perceived political direction of the state" (Moja, Muller & Cloete, 1996, p.148).

I present this chapter in five sections. In the first section, I briefly discuss global university policy-steerage mechanisms. In the second section, I briefly explain the new-managerialism in relation to university governance in Malawi. In the third section, I briefly describe the challenges associated with the new-managerialism in relation to university governance in Malawi. In the fourth section, I show the interventionist nature of university governance in Malawi; and lastly in the fifth section, I present the conclusion.

Global Policy-Steerage and University Governance

The nature of policy-steerage mechanisms in a country influence university governance models (Bleiklie & Kogan, 2007). Policy-steerage models can affect a range of governance issues within the university such as funding, composition of councils and many other educational issues (Taylor & Miroiu, 2002). I briefly look at state control and state supervising policy-steerage models in turn.

The state control model dominated African countries after independence. With this model, university education is directly managed by governments, and universities are part of the general public administration (van Vught, 1994). While in Malawi, among other countries, this model developed into negative control of universities by the government (Habib, Morrow & Bentley, 2008; Kerr & Mapanje, 2002), the model ought not to be necessarily negative. This model is characterised by strong dependency on government funding and decisions (Gornitzka, 1999) and it is useful in terms of achieving university education that contributes to national growth, a view which has been advanced by African leaders generally (Moja, et al., 1996).

Studies on African university management and governance (Gaidzanwa, 1994; Saint, 2009) show the following key features of the state control model: the dominance of the government of the day through the Ministry of Education; a system of university council, senate and a university administration headed by a vice-chancellor with deans heading faculties; use of acts of parliaments and availability of university councils that are mandated with managing the universities. While most of these features characterise universities in Malawi (Mzuzu University, 1997; The University of Malawi, 1998) in terms of policy dictates, one needs to note that practically the governance system is or has been very interventionist. I shall return to this later.

The state supervisory university policy-steerage model is different from state control as it allows more freedom to universities to decide their goals and stresses institutional autonomy (Gornitzka, 1999). Taylor and Miroiu (2002) argue that this model, also called the new managerialism, is oriented to the market and that most European countries are moving towards it. The following characterise the state supervisory model: withdrawal of governments from control functions; formation of buffer bodies such as councils for higher education; developing funding models that give flexibility to institutions to diversify sources of income; formation of quality assurance and accountability systems, affirmation of the university governing board as accountable to the minster or buffer body, and gradual withdrawal of the state from direct decision-making on the appointment of the university council chairpersons (Fielden, 2008; Saint, 2009). There is evidence of a steady move towards the new managerialism in Malawi's university governance.

New Managerialism and University Governance in Malawi

I start by briefly explaining the African scenario as well as the global changes as far as university governance is concerned. As noted, while African university education may have been chiefly characterised by the state control model, newer legal frameworks for university education reflect international trends of the state supervisory model (the new managerialism). While neoliberalism and the new managerialism are not necessarily homologous notions, they influence each other and this idea is well captured by Olssen and Peters (2005) who posit that:

> A further consequence of marketisation has been the increased emphasis on performance and accountability assessment, with accompanying use of performance indicators and personal appraisal systems. This has generated a concern with corporate loyalty and the use of discipline against employees who criticise their universities. Universities in this model have become concerned with their market reputation and become increasingly intolerant of adverse criticism

of the institution by the staff. Such policies are the logical outcome of privatisation: in the private sector employers are not permitted to criticise their employer in public. Under neoliberalism corporativisation, many universities are employing advertising and public relations agencies to ensure that only positive statements appear about the university and its products. (Olssen & Peters, 2005, pp. 327–328)

As a result, globally, the intellectual oriented university that facilitates free deliberative and collegial governance seems to be replaced by a neoliberal associated form of governance (Davies, Gottsche, & Bansel, 2006; Hall, 2005). New managerialism adheres to a need for quality assurance, performativity, audit cultures, strategic planning and general assessment tools which follow the dictates of the knowledge economy and convey a need to align university education to the needs of the industry (Olssen & Peters, 2005).

Saint (2009) argues that in revising legal frameworks, sub-Saharan African governments tend to follow international trends such as those propelled by the World Bank and that, as such, African universities have embarked on restructuring university governance to reflect the demands of the global neoliberal orthodoxy and the knowledge economy.

Following on the trend, policy documents in Malawi such as the Policy and Investment Framework and the National Education Sector Plan established a basis for quality assurance mechanisms, including policy guidance and accountability systems (Malawi Government, 2006). Currently, the Malawi government and the university sector have set up a Malawi Council for Higher Education following a report on higher education policy assessment (Hayward & Ncayiyana, 2006). The Malawi Council for Higher Education is mandated to facilitate coordination of public universities, approve the registration of new institutions, recommend quality assurance mechanisms, review university governance and strengthen transparency and accountability mechanisms (Malawi Government, 2006).

I contend that the new trends in Malawi reflect a sense of corporatism. For example, the Policy and Investment Framework proposes the following policy directions for higher education financing in Malawi: that tertiary institutions are required to promote cost-effective use of available resources, devise strategies to enhance their capacity to diversify their revenue sources and to introduce appropriate cost-sharing mechanisms aimed at reducing government's subvention for higher education (Malawi Government, 2000). Taken together, it is clear that these policy propositions reflect a move towards the new managerialism of university governance in Malawi. Since in Africa these mechanisms are generally steered by global forces, which show legitimised authority, they seem to be easily incorporated into the African university education without any critical assessment (Samoff & Carrol, 2004). I contend that countries such as Malawi seem to be entangled in blind policy-borrowing.

Challenges of the New Managerialism in University Governance

While in Malawi university policy shows a need for collegial governance, the steady move towards the neoliberal trends obscures efforts for collegial or democratic governance and citizenship education as universities begin to run like industry (Beckmann & Cooper, 2004; Delanty, 2003). More so, the new managerialism encourages universities to concentrate on producing skills required by the labour market at the expense of critical reflections required to build democratic societies (Giroux, 2003). I contend that given the challenges associated with ethnicity, regionalism, patronage politics and others in Malawi, it is dangerous for an education system to ignore a need for greater democratic and citizenship education.

I further hold that neoliberal trends will eventually impede democratic university governance in Malawi as they are based on a performative and monitoring culture that resembles business models. In fact, with these trends, university chancellors in Malawi are expected to conduct their duties as business chief executives, thus impeding their educational duties (Marginson, 2002).

Davies et al., (2005) use a Foucauldian idea of governmentality (the silent or uncritical acceptance to be governed in particular ways) to argue that neoliberal views employed in the new managerialism in university education are posited as the unquestioned in demanding academics, for example, to be loyal to vice chancellors whose job is to run universities as chief executives. In employing the new managerialism rhetoric debate within the university is curtailed as it can be viewed as disloyalty to chief executives of the university (Olssen & Peters, 2005).

As such, according to Olssen and Peters (2005), neoliberal governmentality has given rise to shifts from collegial or democratic governance models to imposed management models of powerful-less-powerful chains of command. I argue that the emergence of the market forces in university governance in Malawi will encourage such trends.

Giroux (2003) bemoans these market forces and the new managerialism in university education and governance and posits that:

> Fundamental to the rise of a vibrant democratic culture is the recognition that education must be treated as public good —

> as a crucial site where students gain a public voice and come to grips with their own power as individual and social agents. Public and higher education cannot be viewed merely as sites for commercial investment or for affirming a notion of the private good based exclusively on the fulfilment of individual needs. Reducing higher education to the handmaiden of corporate culture works against the critical social imperative of educating citizens who can sustain and develop inclusive democratic public spheres. (Giroux, 2003, p. 182)

Further, Giroux (2003) contends that new managerialism has brought new ways of governance in which the management model is one that replaces faculty governance (i.e., the community of scholars) with that of the language of accountability which impedes democratic governance. As such, university students are conceptualised as human capital in need of training for paid work at the expense of a broad-based critical pedagogy (Beckmann, Cooper, & Hill, 2009).

Another problem that arises within the new managerialism is the conceptualisation of what it means by knowledge and what type of knowledge universities need to impart (Peters, 2003). Peters further argues that in the age of global capitalism within which new managerialism takes primacy, there are struggles not only over the meaning and value of knowledge but also over the means of knowledge production. For example, Hall (2005) contends that new managerialism has shifted the focus from educational purposes and politics in education to an emphasis on what works. What matters as knowledge, therefore, is that which can be measured; and as such scientific evidence that proves what works is legitimated as knowledge. By implication and following on Peters' (2003) argument, this alters not only what it means by knowledge, but also the ways knowledge is produced and communicated within the university. In the same vein, Hall (2005), poses the question: "what are the policy implications of a policy mission that focuses narrowly on providing solutions to, rather than stimulating ongoing deliberations about educational problems?" (Hall, 2005, p. 182).

It is noted that students prepared for the market only lack the required deliberative mechanisms to engage with the public (Beckmann & Cooper, 2004; Beckmann, et al., 2009; Giroux, 2003). In Malawi, where a need for citizen participation in governance is pertinent following thirty years of dictatorship by Kamuzu Banda from 1964-1994, citizenship education is of paramount importance.

Market forces have been viewed as exacerbating social injustice. In England, for example, studies show that market forces have encouraged inequality in accessing education, resulting into class problems (Beckmann & Cooper, 2004; Beckmann, et al., 2009; Whitty, Power, & Halpin, 1998). Similarly, in Malawi, due to the adherence to market forces, the poor are failing to meet costs for university education generally.

The Interventionist Nature of University Governance in Malawi

In this section, I present my second argument that university governance in Malawi is also hampered by the interventionist nature of policy-steerage by the government. As noted earlier, the interventionist model happens when HEIs become sites of opposition to the development path or perceived political direction of the state. Omari (1991) lists the following features of the interventionist model: an inactive chancellor who is often also the president of the country; a weak Ministry of Education which fails to promote universities; a weak and poorly educated personnel in the higher university planning department; university councils which are largely dormant and only reactive to issues; large senates that solely concentrate on academic issues and vice chancellors who are normally appointed and fired at the pleasure of the state president. These characteristics largely typify the university governance system in Malawi.

For example, in terms of governance structures, the University of Malawi Council comprises the following members: the chairperson appointed by the state president; the vice chancellor; the principals of the constituent colleges; the secretary for education or his designated representative (ex-officio); the secretary to the treasury or his designated representative (ex-officio); two members appointed by the chancellor; one member appointed by the University of Malawi ex-students' association; one member appointed by the council from a panel of three persons distinguished in university affairs in Malawi, nominated by the vice chancellor; one female member and one male member elected by the University of Malawi Students' Union, other members not exceeding four co-opted by the council (The University of Malawi, 1998). This composition is similar to those of other national universities, with minor differences. However, while the composition of the governing bodies in public universities in Malawi shows a balanced composition, this does not mean that decisions are free from interventionist modes of policy-steerage.

Two major issues characterise the intervention model: first, the fact that the state president becomes automatic chancellor of public universities; and second, the president's power in making usually reactive policies despite the fact that he/she ought to be a ceremonial figure. The system of state presidents assuming the position of chancellor of public universities was facilitated by a need to align African universities to national development

(Zeleza, 2003). Historically, this system has been abused especially in Malawi (Kerry & Mapanje, 2002).

As described in the university acts, while the role of the chancellor is meant to be ceremonial (The University of Malawi, 1998), some state presidents in Malawi have tended to garner too much power in governing universities. University vice chancellors and managers have usually tended to support the state presidents' actions for fear of losing jobs. Some university managers tend to blindly support state presidents because they do not want to lose resources that governments provide to the universities. I contend that the role of state presidents as chancellors of public universities militates against the independence of the university and works as a source of oppression.

A major challenge of the interventionist mechanism is shown through policy formulation that tends to follow presidents' own quest to sustain political power. As an example, I briefly discuss the university access policy that shows patronage aspects in Malawi (see Shawa, 2012; 2014).

While many African governments have used, at one point or the other, quotas for university selection, these have generally been premised on rural versus urban or less resourced schools versus more resourced schools (Kwesiga & Ahikire, 2006). In Malawi, however, the premise has been on ethnicity, which means that the region or district of origin takes precedence over whether a candidate studies at a well-resourced school or not. This has made the access policy more complicated in Malawi than in most African countries. Premising it on ethnic lines means that politicians can use the policy to achieve their political goals by, for example, favouring their ethnic or linguistic groupings in accessing university education.

In 1987, President Banda abandoned use of merit in selecting students to the university and introduced a quota policy based on district of origin or ethnicity (Posner, 1995). The implicit argument was that people from the northern region tended to do better that those from other regions using the merit system. While the policy was challenged in court, later President Mutharika (2004-2012) re-introduced the policy amidst several protests. Both presidents used the policy to garner political support or favours as the perceived victims of the policy were the minority ethnicities. In a deliberative university system, one would expect rational decisions that allow for social justice to prevail in university governance.

Conclusion

In this chapter, I have advanced two arguments: First, that university governance in Malawi is being impacted upon negatively by the global neoliberal orthodoxy. Second, that in Malawi university governance is also hampered by the interventionist nature of policy-steerage by the government. Regarding the first argument, I have shown that university policy is responding to the market forces that negatively impact on democratic and citizenship principles of university governance. For the second argument, I have posited that making presidents automatic chancellors of public universities allows for interventionist modes of governance as some presidents have used their statuses to dictate university policy for political gains. The combination of the two challenges poses serious threats to university governance mechanisms in Malawi.

Chapter 11

Organisational Commitment of Academic Staff at Universities in Uganda

Edith Namutebi & John Baptist Mpoza

Introduction

Post-independence university education in East Africa started with the metamorphosis in 1963 of Makerere College, hitherto an affiliate of the University of London, into the University of East Africa — headquartered at Makerere Hill in Kampala and with constituent colleges at Nairobi, Kenya, and Dar es Salaam, Tanzania. Structurally and culturally modelled along Oxbridge, and being born at the beginning of the decade of Africa's political independence — with a crucially important mandate of producing high quality manpower to replace vacating expatriates of the colonial administration in the region — the university offered an elite, hence lavish, work and boarding environment to its staff and students. Academic staff were offered decent accommodation facilities on-campus, competitive pay packages and security of tenure. They were also provided with opportunities for further education and regularly promoted to different ranks of academic seniority. They attended to few students — because the university admitted only 'the cream of the crop', sifted through a highly restrictive pre-university education system. The students were also provided with high quality laboratory and library support in addition to frills accommodation and lavish stipends (Tiberondwa, 1998; Ssekamwa, 1997).

After the split, in 1971, of the University of East Africa into Makerere University, Dar es Salaam University and Nairobi University, however, all these universities were grossly underfunded, by their governments — due to the economic downturn of the 1970s and subsequent adoption in the mid-1980s of IMF/World Bank recommended structural adjustment programmes that discouraged government spending on higher education (Mamdani, 2007). In Uganda, as in many other African countries, this affected Makerere University's potential for quality assurance. Physical resources dilapidated and staff salaries were outstripped by inflation (Mayanja, 1996; Kassam, 1999). At the same time, pressure mounted on the university to expand its student intake, since barely 22% of applicants that were eligible for admission were being accepted yet the institution was the only university in Uganda (PDD, 2000).

To surmount these challenges, government liberalised university education, in line with the IMF/ World Bank recommended structural adjustment programmes of the 1980s. This involved allowing Makerere University, hitherto the preserve of a few state-sponsored students, to admit fee-paying students, who are enrolled in evening, weekend and distance-learning or 'off-campus' study programmes, in addition to the conventional state-sponsored students that are enrolled in day schedule teaching programmes. It also involved allowing the private sector to start universities. Among other benefits, these reforms provided academic staff with an opportunity to improve their incomes. At the public universities, academic staff involved in teaching fee-paying students are paid allowances for teaching the students. Many of these academic staff also conduct part-time teaching at the privately owned universities, usually in proximity to the public universities where they hold their main employment, through which they raise some extra income (Altbach, 2005a).

However, the downside of the developments is that they transformed university education in the country in ways that may distress academic staff. First, they involved many of the staff accepting very heavy teaching loads. From teaching a few students enrolled in day-time schedules, these staff now attend to hundreds of students enrolled in a multiplicity of study programmes at both the public and private universities. Moreover, the staff teach many of these students during anti-social times (e.g. evenings, weekends and holidays) — something that could affect their work-life balance. Incidentally, the expanded number of students came with an equally expanded student coursework, examination and research project supervision load. This is despite the fact that, in addition to teaching and supervising the many students, the staff are expected to attract competitive grants, conduct research, attend conferences, publish articles and books, offer community service relevant to their areas of academic specialisation and accept administrative roles in their departments/universities and professional associations to which they belong. This is in service to their universities' three-track service mandate of teaching, research and community engagement.

Second, it has been argued that, unlike the case with the conventional state-sponsored students, who are selected on the basis of exceptional performance in highly competitive pre-entry examinations and many of whose tuition and non-tuition costs are borne by the state, the learning readiness of many of the fee-paying students is low. It has been argued that many of the fee-paying students are not as academically apt as the conventional state-sponsored students; live on meagre budgets for procurement of both tuition and non-tuition requirements; and are disoriented from the studious nature of academic work. Many of them divide their time between part-time employment and study, the inference being that their lecturers and professors find them more difficult to teach.

At the same time, since the late 1980s, the academic staff have made incessant complaints about their remuneration and facilitation, the contribution of the reforms to the improvement of the same notwithstanding (see, e.g., Jaramogi, 2013; Kagolo, 2013; Kayongo, 2013). Specifically, the staff contend that, over time, their monetary benefits have been outstripped by inflation. Moreover, for a host of reasons, most of the staff are no longer provided with accommodation, so they spend part of their meagre pay on accommodation and also succumb to the difficulties involved in commuting to and from work. An apparent consequence of the inadequacy of the staff's monetary benefits is that, in addition to their heavy teaching load at both the public and private universities, many of them moonlight in activities such as private consultancy, teaching in secondary schools and trading businesses. Regarding facilitation, authors such as Yawe (2010), Mugizi (2007) and Tamale (2007) show that the staff have complained that, among other problems, they are not provided with quality ICT facilities and support (notably Internet connectivity); laboratory equipment; library resources (notably subscription to relevant journals); scholarships; funding towards research and travel; and basic office facilities such as stationery. The staff have also complained about a degenerated working environment — citing such problems as congestion in teaching and office areas; dilapidation of physical structures; and outages of essential supplies such as electricity and running water for toilet use!

Most of the private universities in the country also typify these problems, apparently because they have been closely modelled along, and are significantly influenced by, the public universities in their proximity. Moreover, concerns have also been expressed that, in addition to these anomalies, the private universities are characterised by particularly precarious conditions of facilitation and exhibit sloppy management practices, including disregard for conventional academic staff management practices such as meritorious selection, regular promotion to seniority and stability of tenure. In these universities, concerns have been expressed that some of these anomalies are the consequence of the universities' pursuit of profit, which is not adequately regulated by the NCHE and relevant accreditation agencies.

This being the case, a question relating to quality assurance in the universities comes to mind: are the academic staff of these universities committed to the universities and their work? The significance of the question stems from the fact that commitment is about maintaining membership in an organisation with the intention of contributing to its success (Meyer et al., 2007; Cetin, 2006) — a key prerequisite for the universities' development — albeit the challenges in the universities described above could demoralise the academic staff. However, review of related literature leads to the conclusion that, hitherto, this question had not attracted scholarly attention. This chapter reports on the findings of a study that undertook to respond to the question.

Research Framework

To investigate the academic staff's organisational commitment, reference was made to earlier studies on the subject — to construct a framework within whose orientation pertinent variables may be identified and conceptualised. Review of the studies shows that they concur that organisational commitment is to be defined as an employee's psychological attachment to his/her employing organisation and that this commitment is characterised by: 1) an intention to continue working in the organisation; 2) identification with the organisation's values and goals; and 3) a willingness to exert extra effort with the view to bring benefit to the organisation. Meyer and Allen's (1990) three-component model (TCM), enumerates three dimensions of organisational commitment: affective, continuance and normative. Several studies endorse the applicability of this model to the study of organisational commitment. Thus, investigation of the commitment of academic staff in universities in Uganda focused on attributes of the model.

According to Veličković et al. (2014), affective commitment expresses itself in an employee's emotional attachment to his/ her organisation and its goals. It is a result of congruence between an employee's and the organisation's cherished values and goals (Jaros, 2007). Employees who are affectively committed to their organisations believe in the organisations' goals (Kanning & Hill, 2014) and are willing to maintain their membership with the organisations (van Dick & Ullrich, 2013; Dirani & Kuchinke, 2011). Affective commitment is expressed not only in form of clear understanding of and identification with an organisation but also in form of satisfaction with membership to the organisation and demonstration of competence (Ahmad & Oranye, 2010).

The level of affective commitment is determined by employee- and organisation-based factors. Employee factors include self-interest, interpersonal relations, value and goal orientation, personal belief in the organisation's values and goals, education, age, marital status, degree of family responsibility, seniority, sense of job security, job satisfaction and comfort, and availability and attractiveness of alternatives (Antón, 2009; Hulpia et al., 2009; Vandenberghe, Bentein & Stinglhamber, 2004; O'Malley, 2000). Organisational factors include: clarity of employees' roles, clarity of performance targets, management support, remuneration, design of work environment, organisation's reputation, and career development opportunities provided (Chang et al., 2007; Meyer et al., 2007). Affective commitment also depends on a match between what an employee expects and is looking for in a job, and what the job provides. Other factors include how employees are inducted. According to Mignerey et al. (1995), well-inducted employees display higher levels of affective organisational commitment because they feel well prepared, more familiar with, and at ease within, the organisation. They are also more receptive to feedback and other interventions that encourage social integration.

The level of affective commitment also depends on the quality of the relationship between managers and their employees. Employees who enjoy good relationships with their immediate managers or who are fairly treated by management, especially in terms of the policies pursued, promotions, participation in decision making, and remuneration have greater affective commitment (Mguqulwa, 2008; CIPD, 2001; Meyer, 1997; Green et al., 1996; Settoon et al., 1996). This commitment is also affected by the quality of relationships at the workplace (Baumeister & Leary, 1995). Positive collegial interaction is rewarding, since it strengthens feelings of belonging that bind employees to the organisation (Baumeister & Leary, 1995). Another factor that affects affective commitment is the balance between home and work (Wayne et al., 2013). Employees with the right balance between home and work are more committed than those lacking this balance. Home-work balance is achieved where there are flexible work arrangements, time-off policies, paid leaves, arrangements for childcare, elderly care, healthcare, provision of family support information and counselling, and convenience services, amongst other services (Dello Russo et al., 2013; Wayne et al., 2013).

Continuance commitment defines the cognitive attachment of an employee to his/her employing organisation, which is occasioned by a tendency to avoid costs an employee incurs as a result of leaving the organisation (Allen & Meyer, 1990; Meyer et al., 2012). The higher the commitment of the employees, the greater the costs of changing. Similarly, the lower this commitment becomes, the more the benefits of leaving an organisation outweigh the incurred costs (Gutierrez, Candel & Carver, 2012; Cetin, 2006). The costs may be in the form of loss of salary or wages, loss of networks and contacts, loss of other benefits such as access to ICT facilities, and loss of identity and prestige (Dirani & Kuchinke, 2011; Ahmad & Oranye, 2010). Other costs include job search expenses, inconvenience in relocation, loss of investment in non-transferable assets (e.g. skills that are unique to a particular organisation) and working relationships with co-workers that make it too costly for one to leave an organisation (McMahon, 2009; Allen, 2003). The other cause of continuance commitment is the employee's perceived lack of better alternatives outside of an organisation (Shahanwaz & Juyal, 2006; Camilleri, 2002; Ugboro, & Obeng, 2001). Indeed, if there are no readily available employment opportunities outside of their organisations, the costs of leaving current organisations are invariably higher and lead to a stronger sense of continuance commitment. Davila and Garcia (2012) indicate that the older employees become, the less alternative employment options are available to them. As a result, older employees display higher levels of continuance commitment. Dunham et al. (1994) indicate that older employees tend to display higher levels of normative commitment because the organisation has invested in them much more than in their young counterparts.

On the other hand, normative commitment delineates a feeling of obligation to remain with an organisation (Gutierrez et al., 2012; Fridoon & Nasrin, 2009; Allen & Meyer, 1990). Employees think that they ought to remain with an organisation because they think it is the morally right thing to do (Balfour & Wechsler, 1996). Normative commitment occurs especially when the organisation has considerably contributed to employees' career development by offering scholarships and training or increasing their social capital through sponsored exposure (Jackson, Meyer & Wang, 2013; Green et al.,1996; Baumeister & Leary, 1995).

Investigation of the commitment of academic staff in Uganda was informed by the findings of the aforementioned studies. Data was collected using the organisational commitment questionnaire developed by Allen and Meyer (1990) — from a sample of 384 academic staff who were drawn from a population of 136,002 (see, Education Statistical Abstract, 2010). The academic staff were selected from eleven (11) universities using convenience selection techniques. The questionnaire was modified to suit the context of the study. The respondents' views were elicited using a 5-point Likert scale running from "totally disagree" (1), through "disagree" (2), "undecided" (3) and "agree" (4), to "totally agree" (5) with a given statement on the respondent's organisational commitment. The data was analysed using means and percentages.

Findings and Discussion

Table 11.1 shows the respondents' mean scores on attributes of organisational commitment.

Table 11.1: Mean Scores on Attributes of Organisational Commitment (N = 380)

Attributes of Organisational Commitment		Category of University		
		Public	Religious	Independent
Affective	I would be very happy to spend the rest of my career with the university	4.41	4.05	3.67
	I enjoy talking about my university with people outside	3.56	3.55	3.54
	I feel as if the university's problems are my own	4.39	3.53	3.61
	I think that I could not easily become as attached to another organisation as I am to this university	3.86	3.79	3.54
	I feel like a part of family at the university	3.85	3.95	3.56
	I feel 'emotionally attached' to the university	4.38	4.11	3.74
	The university has a great deal of meaning for me	4.30	3.96	3.57
	I feel a strong sense of belonging to university	3.67	3.79	3.59
	Total	**4.05**	**3.84**	**3.60**
(Continued)				
Continuance	I am afraid of what might happen if I quit my job without having another one lined up	4.91	4.67	4.55
	It would be very hard for me to leave my university right now, even if I wanted to	4.86	4.65	4.53
	Too much in my life would be disrupted if I decided to leave the university now	4.79	4.61	4.50

	It is too costly for me to leave the university	4.86	4.79	4.54
	Right now, staying with the university is a matter of necessity as much as desire	4.88	4.95	4.56
	I feel that I have very many options to consider before leaving the university	4.68	4.74	4.61
	One of the few serious consequences of leaving this university is scarcity of alternatives	4.90	4.66	4.57
	I continue working for the university because leaving requires huge personal sacrifice	4.87	4.79	4.59
	Total	**4.83**	**4.73**	**4.56**
	(Continued)			
Normative	I think people these days move from company to company too often	3.57	3.76	3.55
	I believe a person must always be loyal to his or her employing organisation	3.88	3.96	3.54
	Jumping from organisation to organisation seems unethical to me	4.33	3.76	4.15
	One of the major reasons I continue to work in this university is that I believe loyalty is vital – I feel a sense of moral obligation to remain	3.67	3.91	3.53
	If I got another offer for a better job elsewhere I would not feel it is right to leave the university	3.62	3.71	3.51
	I was taught to believe in the value of remaining loyal to one organisation	3.91	3.71	3.61

		Things were better in the days when people stayed in one organisation for most of their careers	3.55	3.61	4.14
		I do not think that to be a university academic staff is sensible anymore	4.19	3.56	4.13
		Total	3.84	3.75	3.77
	Grand Total		**4.20**	**4.08**	**4.01**

The mean scores in Table 11.1 were all close to '4' and '5' (respectively corresponding to "agree" and "totally agree" on the Likert scale used). This implies that the academic staff were organisationally committed to their universities. A more critical analysis of the magnitudes of the mean values reveals that while most of them were close to '4', those corresponding to continuance commitment were close to '5'. This implies that the level of the academic staff's continuance commitment to universities was higher than their level of affective and normative commitment. A scrutiny of the magnitudes of the mean values reveals that regarding the type, academic staff in public universities were generally more organisationally committed than their counterparts in private universities. The magnitudes of the mean values corresponding to foundation body reveal the same thing. They also indicate that academic staff in religious-founded universities were generally more committed than their counterparts in universities founded by independent secular private bodies.

When considered from the point of view articulated by Meyer et al. (2007) and Cetin (2006), among other authors, these findings suggest that the universities are optimally benefiting from their academic staff. Indeed, as these authors argue, being organisationally committed implies that employees are contributing to the success of their organisation by not quitting or absenting from work, but by identifying with the organisation's goals and values and performing all assigned work to the extent of even putting in extra effort to find more creative and productive ways of improving the organisation's performance.

The findings in Table 11.1 indicate that the level of the academic staff's organisational commitment was heterogeneous. The dons' affective and normative commitment was not as strong as their continuance commitment. This suggests that the academics' commitment was more as a result of cognitive attachment to their universities. According to Allen and Meyer (1990) this kind of organisational attachment is not occasioned by love for the organisation and a desire to ensure that it succeeds. It is also not the type of commitment that would make the academic staff work in appreciation of what the universities had invested in them. It is commitment motivated by fear of costs that an employee has to incur if he or she chooses to leave his or her current university. This was substantiated by the reasons that the academics gave in support of their commitment to their universities (Table 11.2).

Table 11.2: Reasons Cited for Remaining in Employing University (%, N = 380)

Reason	%
Personal identification as a university academic staff	23.7
Opportunity to win and conduct paid research using free university facilities	18.4
Opportunity to conduct personal research using free university facilities	15.8
Access to sponsored career development/training opportunities	14.7
Lack of alternative gainful employment opportunities in the job market	65.8
Limited market for the wealth of knowledge acquired over a long period	7.90
Guaranteed job security	21.1

Loss of free access to recreational services	11.3
Loss of secure accommodation	8.70
Guilty to leave after the university's heavy investment in my training	14.5
I am too old to think of shifting to another organisation	14.2
The university provides enough time for balancing work and family affairs	26.3
Non-pecuniary benefits the university provides far outweigh the meagre salary	52.6
I enjoy teaching university students, irrespective of what I earn from it	23.7
Prestige associated with being a university academic staff	26.6

Note: Multiple responses were elicited

Table 11.2 shows that when asked about their reasons for remaining in their universities, most of the academic staff cited reasons that are associated with the benefits their universities provided and the costs they might incur if they chose to leave the universities. These findings suggest that the universities are at a risk of losing their academic staff, since the academic staff would leave once the benefits of their leaving outweigh the associated costs (cf. Gutierrez et al., 2012). As such, it is concluded that the universities need to strengthen their academic staff's affective and normative commitment. The findings in Table 11.1 reveal that the academic staff's organisational commitment varied significantly and in such a way that it was generally higher at public universities than at private universities, especially those that were founded by secular private bodies. This implies that efforts to improve affective and normative organisational commitment are more needed at private than at public universities.

Chapter 12

Viability of Open Educational Resources in Open and Distance Learning: Views of Members of the Executive Board of the African Council for Distance Education, Kenya

Vincent Ado Tenebe & Rotimi Ogidan

Introduction

Nations seek to provide quality education for all their citizens in an equitable and accessible manner. However, for a host of reasons, conventional approaches to educational development and delivery have excluded some groups of people from educational programmes. The need to include these groups in educational programmes has created a need for a radical departure from the conventional approaches to educational delivery, in which access to educational materials is closed to one in which these materials are availed in the public domain. As well, open and distance learning (ODL) is seen as an option for including these groups in educational programmes. However, ODL is not without challenges. It involves the dilemma of expanding access and improving quality, on one hand, while using ever-reducing funds and other forms of facilitation, on the other. Confronting this challenge requires adoption of open educational resources

(OERs) as a strategy for achieving cheaper and faster production and dissemination of knowledge (D'Antoni, 2009). This is especially so given the emergence of ICT innovations and a tech-savvy generation of learners who are not restricted to the physical classroom (Mushi & Muganda, 2011).

Concept and Potential of OERs

OERs are teaching, learning, and research resources that reside in the public domain or have been released under an intellectual property license that permits their free use and/or re-purposing. They include modules, textbooks, videos, tests, software, and other materials that are used to support access to information (William & Flora Hewlett Foundation, 2008; OECD, 2007; Mushi & Muganda, 2011). OERs can be regarded as a concept and as a movement. According to Mushi and Muganda (2011), the concept of OERs that was invented at the 2002 UNESCO forum on the impact of open courseware on HEIs in developing countries originated from the open courseware developed at Massachusetts Institute of Technology in the 1990s. In the 21st century, the concept of OERs has expanded to include teaching, learning and research materials developed for public consumption.

OERs are grounded in the understanding of education as a common good with the ethos of ODL, which is analogous to a philosophy of openness. Education as a common good relates to democratisation of access to knowledge that was promoted by philosophers such as John Dewey and Michael Young. Thus, the OERs approach to the delivery of educational programmes is guided by non-commercial and non-monopolistic principles. OERs give expression to the philosophic conception of open learning articulated for the Open University of United Kingdom by Lord Crowther as an approach to learning that is free to people, content, place, methods and tools (Crowther, 1969). Users of

OERs are free to adopt, modify and redistribute educational resources according to the agreements expressed under respective licenses. One of the major strengths of the OERs approach is its ubiquity across disciplines and ability to be disseminated online and through traditional media (i.e. print, CD-ROM, artefacts and the performing arts).

Tremendous support for the growth of OERs can be found in the activities of UNESCO (2002), OECD (2007), Cape Town Open Education Declaration (2008), William and Flora Hewlett Foundation (2008) and D'Antoni (2009). Since the introduction of the OERs approach to educational delivery, different forms of OERs have emerged, including courseware, content and study programmes. Consortia for OERs have also emerged and most recently, there has been formation of the OER University (Wikieducator, 2011). Teacher education in sub-Saharan Africa (TESSA) materials, which were developed by a consortium of experts in teacher education with the view to assist in the provision of quality teacher education, can also be freely downloaded, adapted, translated and integrated with other materials in programmes for teacher education (TESSA, 2011).

The use of OERs in ODL institutions is seen as crucial. According to Peratton, Robinson and Creed (2001), OERs in ODL constitute processes by which a significant proportion of teaching can be conducted through a strategy that surmounts the constraints of space and time. Indeed, in a way, OER is synonymous to ODL because OERs are often the most cost-effective means of maximising the ratio of outcomes to inputs (Hulsmann, 2000).

OERs are aimed at using ICT to try to equalise access to knowledge and educational opportunities across the world. As an approach to the delivery of educational programmes, they target educators and students worldwide and their use is hoped to open access to education and free learners from the constraints of time and place (UNESCO, 2002). By using OERs, learners are disposed to flexible learning opportunities as individuals and as groups. Indeed, the approach is designed to enable people to learn from the convenience of their homes and/or workplaces. OERs also provide opportunity for the use of technology in teaching and learning. If teachers and learners in ODL are separated by time and space, then the use of OERs would be an appropriate strategy to achieve cost-effective learning. Integration of OERs in ODL institutions is also hoped to enhance opportunities for HEIs to cooperate in improving the quality of teaching and learning.

Questions and Approach

Despite the advantages with which OERs are associated, their viability in ODL will depend on a number of factors: 1) the way leaders of ODL institutions understand these resources and the benefits with which they are associated; 2) the willingness of academic staff to integrate the resources into their work; and 3) institutional policies that favour the development and utilisation of the resources.

With a membership of 40 HEIs (Table 12.1), the ACDE is working to promote research, policy and quality in ODL, so as to increase access to education and training in Africa (cf. Ogidan & Sanusi, 2011).

Table 12.1: ACDE Member Institutions

SN	Institutions Registered with ACDE	Mode of Course Delivery
1	African Virtual University	Distance
2	Anambra State University	Dual Mode
3	Botswana College of Distance and Open Learning	Distance
4	Copperbelt University	Dual Mode
5	Eduardo Mondlane University	Dual Mode
6	Egerton University	Dual Mode

7	El. Neelain University	Dual Mode
8	Federal University of Technology Minna	Dual Mode
9	Institute Superior Pendago	Dual Mode
10	Jomo Kenyatta University of Agriculture and Technology	Dual Mode
11	Kenya School of law	Dual Mode
12	Kenyatta University	Dual Mode
13	Laweh Open University College, Ghana	Distance
14	Marien Ngouabi University	Dual Mode
15	Maseno University	Dual Mode
16	Masinde Muliro University	Dual Mode
17	Moi University	Dual Mode
18	Mulungushi University	Dual Mode
19	National Open University of Nigeria	Distance
20	National Teachers' Institute, Nigeria	Distance
21	North West University	Dual Mode
22	Open university of Sudan	Distance
23	Open University of Mauritius	Distance
24	Open University of Tanzania	Distance
25	Plasma University	Dual Mode
26	Strathmore University	Dual Mode
27	Tumaini University Uni	Dual Mode
28	University of Ibadan	Dual Mode
29	University of Juba	Dual Mode
30	University of Lagos	Dual Mode
31	University of Maiduguri	Dual Mode
32	University of Nairobi	Dual Mode
33	University of Ngaoundere	Dual Mode
34	University of Pretoria	Dual Mode
35	University of Rwanda	Dual Mode
(Continued)		
36	University of South Africa (UNISA)	Distance
37	University of Zambia	Dual Mode
38	University of Abuja	Dual Mode
39	Zambian Open University	Distance
40	Zimbabwean Open University	Distance

Pursuant to this mission, members of the council's executive board (Table 12.2) discussed the OERs approach to the delivery of educational programmes – with the view to gain insights into its viability in ODL in Africa.

Table 12.2: Members of the Executive Board of ACDE

Member	Designation in ACDE
Executive Director (ACDE)	Ex-Officio
Vice Chancellor, Open University of Tanzania	President
Vice Chancellor, University of Abuja, Nigeria	1st Vice President
Vice Chancellor, Al-Neelain University, Sudan	2nd Vice President
Vice Chancellor, Egerton University	Secretary General
Vice Chancellor, University of South Africa	Treasurer
Vice Chancellor, National Open University of Nigeria	Representative of West African Region
Vice Chancellor, Kenyatta University	Representative of East African Region
Vice Chancellor, Zimbabwe Open University	Representative of Southern African Region
Vice Chancellor, Open University of Sudan	Representative of Northern African Region
Director, Faculty of Pharmaceutical Sciences, University of Kinshasa	Representative of Francophone Countries
Secretary General of the Association of African Universities	Co-opted Member
Director of Quality Assurance and Accreditation Agency (ACDE)	Co-opted Member
Director of Technical Committee on Collaboration (ACDE)	Co-opted Member
Director of ICT (ACDE)	Co-opted Member
Director of ACDE Database (ACDE)	Co-opted Member

Attention was paid to three specific questions:

- How well do leaders of ODL institutions appreciate the scope of OERs and the benefits that they offer?
- To what extent would leaders of ODL institutions affirm that the academic staff of their institutions are prepared to integrate OERs in their work?
- To what extent would leaders of ODL institutions affirm that their institutions' policies favour the development and deployment of OERs?

The responses of the members of the executive board of ACDE to these questions were taken to be significant because the board is constituted by senior members of the council's secretariat and leaders of HEIs where ODL is a major or sole mode of delivery (cf. Table 12.1), the inference being that they may be particularly knowledgeable about ODL.

Viability of OERs in ODL in Africa

The respondents were knowledgeable about OERs albeit to varying degrees. Some of them knew about OERs and their benefits and were already using them in their institutions. The second category knew about the benefits of the resources but had not adopted them yet in their institutions. The other participants, who were the minority, had heard about the resources but did not have a clear understanding of their scope and the benefits they offer.

The participants who knew about OERs were optimistic about the acceptability of the OERs approach to the academic staff of their institutions. These noted that using OERs would promote quality assurance, since learning materials would be placed in the public domain where they might be meaningfully critiqued. Nevertheless, it was also noted that some of the academic staff worry about inadequacies in their materials being exposed if they are distributed as OERs. Indeed, some of the participants explained that, due to concerns for the quality of their work, some of their academic staff did not readily embrace the concept of OERs.

Concerns were also expressed for intellectual property, with arguments being that some of the academic staff worry about losing their materials without being compensated for the same. Moreover, some of the participants also noted that ODL institutions that are generating funds from the sale of study materials to distance learners will lose income if they subscribe as OERs the materials they are currently selling to their students.

Regarding the amenability of pertinent policies to the OERs approach, the general view expressed was that, in many HEIs in Africa, current policy provisions constrain the possible development and utilisation of OERs. This finding is understandable, considering that the policies were developed when the HEIs were elitist (i.e. between the 1940s and 1970s) or during the 1980s and 1990s when HEIs were expanding their student intake albeit with the view to generate critically required income from the sale of educational programmes and resources (cf. Altbach, 2005; Mamdani, 2007).

These findings suggest that institutional policy and financial constraints as well as concerns for quality assurance and intellectual property are affecting adoption of the OERs approach to the delivery of ODL programmes on the continent. This is ironical, considering that the OERs approach is associated with lower costs, simplified access to better quality resources for both faculty and students and that the approach is grounded on non-commercial principles, which put out concerns for intellectual property. Carefully considered, therefore, the aforementioned constraints point to erroneous consideration of the OERs approach, the way it works and the benefits that it offers. Successful adoption of the approach will require review of relevant institutional policies and practices. However, this will require that the leaders and staff of ODL institutions embrace the philosophy of openness and education as a common good, which underpins the OERs approach. In turn, this will require sensitisation of these leaders and staff about OERs.

Chapter 13

Stereotype Threat and University of Botswana Teacher Trainees' Attitude towards their Training Programme and Teaching

H. Johnson Nenty, Phuti Fiji & Moyo Sello

Introduction

Teaching is the first among all nation-building professions. Members of all other professions were 'built' or trained by teachers, and yet teaching is among the least rewarded professions, especially when it comes to intrinsic rewards. In status, it is said to be inferior, and to Shaw (1903, cited in Ihme & Moller, 2015, p. 1), "he who can does, he who cannot teaches". Relegation of teaching affects the motivation of teachers. Stereotype threat, as provoked by the influence of feelings of lowliness, is explained by Ihme and Moller (2015) as a situational threat that diminishes performance due to a negative stereotype about one's own group. In connection to career stereotype, the teaching profession is no exception. Although teaching is labelled as a profession, when compared to other professions such as medicine, engineering and law, teaching scoops off low esteem (Ihme & Moller, 2015). Teacher training programmes have been faced with a decline in enrolment due to a number of factors, including negative stereotype of the teaching profession (Freedberge, 2013).

Maliki (2013) indicates that evidently because of the low status of teaching, candidates in Nigeria choose teacher training programmes as the last resort. When allowing the teaching profession to decline, you get a self-perpetuating future that goes downwards because "good people don't go into it, and those who do go in don't find it satisfying" (Maliki, 2013, p. 12). Societies, including teachers themselves, advise young ones not to go into the teaching profession.

There has also been negative publicity about the teaching profession. One may have the cognitive prowess, knowledge and skill but lacks intrinsic motivation and a favourable attitude towards teaching and these impact on one's teaching competence.

Stereotype threat demotivates and affects what one can do. It also affects commitment to duty and professional development (Nenty, 2010). The teaching profession demands a clear set of goals, and a favourable attitude towards the profession. The teacher's attitude is an important variable in classroom application of new ideas and novel approaches to instruction.

Background

Historically, in Botswana, training of primary school teachers was the responsibility of teacher training colleges. The initial primary school teacher training institution was in Kanye which later relocated to Lobatse (Major & Tiro, 2012). Major and Tiro (2012) further explain that in the 1960s two teacher training colleges were opened in Serowe village and Francistown. These institutions provided certificate and diploma level training programmes. However, the colleges admitted Standard Seven leavers and junior certificate failures, thus teacher education was of low quality

(Major & Tiro, 2012). After Botswana gained independence, quality education was a priority. To improve the quality of teacher education, a government commission recommended raising the quality of entrants to the teaching profession from junior certificate failures to those who passed junior certificate.

Training of teachers was later made a part of the business of University of Botswana, which developed programmes for training teachers up to degree level and further up to higher degrees including Master's and PhD. Although teaching was once more of a masculine career and was valued, it is now known to be more female-oriented, with low wages and motivation. Today, the teaching profession is no longer as attractive to many people as it was in the past and a career stereotype has been built against the profession. This stereotype catches up with pre-service teacher trainees and builds a negative attitude towards the teaching profession among them. Maliki (2013) observes that students accept admission letters from the Faculty of Education for the sake of not staying home. Such students could end up performing poorly or dropping out of the training programme. It is against this background that this study investigated University of Botswana teacher trainees' stereotype threat and attitudes towards their training programme and teaching.

Theoretical Foundation

Stereotypes are shared beliefs, most often derogatory, about a phenomenon or members of a given group, ignoring individual differences. DeRouin, Fritzsche and Salsa (2003) elaborate that members of the stereotyped group become concerned, upset and agitated. Stereotype threat refers to being at risk of confirming, as a self-characteristic, a negative stereotype about one's own social group (Steele, 1997). Steele elaborates that there is evidence pointing to reduced cognitive capacity in mediating the effects of stereotype threat on complex cognitive processing tasks. Stereotype threat involves the cognitive and affective processes that work to drain capacity needed for successful performance. DeRouin, Fritzsche and Salsa (2003) explain that stereotype threat undermines academic achievement by interfering with performance on mental tasks. Over time, stereotype threat promotes victims' attempt to protect their self-esteem by disguising from the threatened domain. This fear tends to impair performance relevant to the stereotype.

Venable (2015) enunciates that culture is one of the factors that influence career choice. Beliefs shared by groups often shape our values and expectations, including career. They hold a shared schema that trickles down to individual level. Performance can be undermined because of the concerns that possibly confirm negative stereotype about teaching as a career.

Bandura's social cognitive career theory stressed by Mills (2009) proposes that career choice is influenced by the beliefs that an individual develops and refines through four major sources: a) personal performance accomplishments, b) vicarious learning, c) social persuasion, and d) physiological states and reactions. The theory stipulates that self-confidence influences successful outcome expectations. Different activities are attempted through a person's educational career, but generally a persistent interest is only developed in activities in which the person expects to be successful and in which a positive outcome is anticipated (Lent & Brown, 2006).

Problem and Purpose of the Study

The extent to which teacher trainees consciously or unconsciously imbibe others' negative perceptions about teaching as a career tends to affect their training and teaching-related behaviour. This inhibits maximum exhibition of behaviour desirable for achievement by teachers and this turns around to hurt the society which, in the first place, maintains a negative view of teaching as a career. Academic under-performance of groups that face negative stereotypes is well documented (DeRouin, Fritzsche & Salsa, 2003). To Nenty (2010), stereotyping a profession tends to undermine both the cognitive and affective dispositions of the members of that profession in carrying out what is required of them. Belittling the teaching profession has led to low enrolment, dropping out and poor performance in teacher training programmes (Maliki, 2010). Career stereotype on teaching has brought about negative attitude, leading to poor competence in the profession.

The purpose of this study was to determine the level of stereotype threat among University of Botswana teacher trainees and its influence on the latter's attitude towards their training programme and teaching. To achieve this, the following hypotheses were tested:

- To University of Botswana teacher trainees, teaching is a significantly stereotyped career.
- The level to which University of Botswana teacher trainees perceive teaching as a stereotyped profession significantly influences:
  a) Their motivation to achieve in their teacher training programme;
  b) Their attitude towards their training programme;
  c) The value they attach to their training programme;
  d) The effectiveness of the training programme;
  e) Their willingness to teach;
  f) Their attitude towards teaching; and
  g) Their view of teaching as a profession.

Significance

Through providing information with which negative beliefs, attitudes and stereotype threat against careers in teaching may be reduced, the findings of this study will contribute to efforts to enhance the success of teacher training programmes. Hence, the Ministry of Education and Skills Development; Faculty of Education at the University of Botswana and other teacher training institutions may find the study beneficial.

Related Literature

Stereotype Threat and Teaching

According to Ambady, Shih, Kim, and Pittinsky (2001), "a growing body of research indicates that the activation of negative stereotypes can impede cognitive performance in adults, whereas positive stereotypes can facilitate cognitive performance" (p. 385). Teacher and pre-service teachers are subject to considerable negative stereotype (Ihme & Moller, 2015). These authors further explain that teachers, more than other occupational groups, are viewed as less competent, and they are confronted with these negative stereotypes even during their training.

Ihme and Moller carried out a study in which a sample of 264 pre-service teachers were randomly divided into three groups. An experiment involving exposure of the third group to stereotype threat was then carried out to test the hypothesis that competence-related stereotype threat leads to weaker performance by pre-service teachers. The study found out that members of the group associated with a negative stereotype posted poorer performance on a test of cognitive ability. This study was well designed, although the researchers could not eliminate the unnoticeable everyday life stereotype and stereotype reactance.

Random assignment of subjects made it suggestible to carry out the study. Howey and Gardner (1983) in the same line of thought with Ihme and Moller (2015) explain that introducing a negative stereotype about a social group in a particular domain tends to reduce the quality of task performance.

A similar study carried out by Nenty (2010) at the University of Botswana determined the level to which stereotype threat was perceived and how it affected students' performance. Data was collected through a 48-item questionnaire which was distributed to 452 teacher trainees. One way ANOVA was used to find out the influence of perceived level of stereotype of teaching as a career on teachers' behaviour. The findings revealed that negative stereotype of the teaching profession affects the performance of teachers during training and at work. It reported that the stereotype view of teaching as a career by Botswana society creates a psychologically hostile working environment within which teachers operate adding that stereotype reduces teachers' cognitive and affective investment into teaching and learning by the teacher and the teacher trainees.

Teacher Trainees' Attitude

Maliki (2013) examined teachers' attitudes towards the teaching profession in Bayelsa State, Nigeria. Carried out as a descriptive survey, a questionnaire was distributed to 150 randomly selected teachers in the state. The finding showed that most teachers had a negative attitude towards teaching and only a few thought of teaching as a humanitarian job. The teachers were not happy since government treated teachers poorly. Teachers expressed low social value of themselves, and felt that they were neither respected nor valued by others in their society. Maliki elaborates that the teachers stressed being dissatisfied with their jobs and would not recommend the profession to any child. However, compared to their male counterparts, female teachers had a more positive attitude towards teaching. Maliki contends that teachers should not be looked down upon by society; rather they should be honoured as *moulders*. She further recommends that the government of Nigeria should enhance teachers' self-image and promote societal attitudinal change through improving teachers' salaries and conditions of service.

Using teachers' attitude inventory administered to 100 B.Ed. teacher trainees, Bhargava and Pathy (2014) investigated the attitude of student teachers towards the teaching profession. The study revealed that female science teachers had more positive attitudes towards teaching than their male counterparts. They also found that new teachers enter teacher training programmes with already established beliefs but pre-service teacher training programmers help in shaping the attitude of teacher trainees by providing a series of experiences incorporated in the curriculum.

A study carried out by Erbas (2014) investigated the relationship between alienation levels of Physical Education teacher candidates and their attitude towards the teaching profession in Turkey. A sample of 695 candidates answered a questionnaire. The teacher trainees felt that the curriculum content did not prepare them for the job. Erbas highlights that alienation and threat can be caused by school administration and academics. He advised that society should develop love for teaching as a career. He also advised that alienation of teaching should be reduced through parental involvement and avoidance of professional isolation of teaching, thereby enhancing some level of admiration for the teaching profession.

Following a normative survey, Mutum (2007) investigated the attitude of teacher trainees towards the teaching profession. The study revealed that 78% of the pre-service students in Imphala East and West campuses of Nagaland University had a positive attitude towards the teaching profession. This finding differs from those of Erbas (2014). However, it concurs with Sharbain and Tan (2012).

Methodology and Findings

Sixty-eight (68) Bachelor of Education and postgraduate diploma in education (PDDE) students were involved in the study. A questionnaire of 54 close-ended items and one open-ended item was used. Section 1 of the questionnaire elicited demographic information about the respondents while Section 2 included closed-ended items with a Likert-type items with 6 options (ranging from very strongly agree to very strongly disagree). Section 3 had open-ended questions. Reliability analysis of the items was carried out.

Hypothesis I

To test the hypothesis that "to University of Botswana teacher trainees, teaching is not a significantly stereotyped career", a t-test analysis of the level to which University of Botswana teacher trainees perceive teaching as a stereotyped career was done. The findings are summarised in Table 13.1.

Table 13.1: Level to which University of Botswana Teacher Trainees Feel that Teaching is a Stereotyped Occupation

(df = 67)

μ	$\bar{X}$	SD	Difference		t-value	Sig.
			Mean	SED		
10.50	12.471	3.216	1.971	0.390	5.053	.000

In Table 13.1, the observed value of t is greater than the corresponding critical at the level of confidence alpha = .05 and corresponding degrees of freedom. Therefore, the null hypothesis was rejected, the inference being that to University of Botswana teacher trainees, teaching is significantly stereotyped.

Hypotheses II

This hypothesis related the level to which University of Botswana teacher trainees perceive teaching as a stereotyped and the trainees' motivation to achieve in their teacher training programme; attitude towards their training programme; the value they attach to their training programme; the effectiveness of the training programme; their willingness to teach; their attitude towards teaching; and their view of teaching as a profession. One-way ANOVA was conducted to test the hypothesis and the findings are summarised in Table 13.2.

Table 13.2: ANOVA in Teacher Trainees' Perception of Teaching and Attitude towards Teacher Training Programme and Teaching

Variable	Level of Stere-otype	n	Mean	SD	SE	Source of Variation	Sum of Squares	df	MS	F	Sig.
Motivation to achieve during teacher training programme	High	16	15.44	2.16	0.54	Between Groups	10.84	2	5.42	1.42	0.25
	Average	32	15.91	2.12	0.37	Within Groups	241.1	63	3.83		
	Low	18	16.56	1.38	0.33	Total	251.94	65			
	Total	66	15.97	1.97	0.24						
Attitude towards teacher training programme	High	18	49	8.51	2	Between Groups	90.35	2	45.18	0.742	0.481
	Average	28	46.96	7.95	1.5	Within Groups	3227.86	53	60.9		
	Low	10	50.1	5.7	1.8	Total	3318.21	55			
	Total	56	48.18	7.77	1.04						
Value attached to teacher training programme	High	16	28.25	3.66	0.92	Between Groups	30.94	2	15.47	0.885	0.418
	Average	32	28.47	4.33	0.77	Within Groups	1031.9	59	17.49		
	Low	14	30.07	4.38	1.17	Total	1062.84	61			
	Total	62	28.77	4.17	0.53						
Effectiveness of Teacher Training Programme	High	16	23.75	4.58	1.15	Between Groups	36.183	2	18.09	0.998	0.374
	Average	32	23.66	4.37	0.77	Within Groups	1160.32	64	18.13		
	Low	19	25.32	3.74	0.86	Total	1196.51	66	18.09		
	Total	67	24.15	4.26	0.52						
Willingness to Teach	High	14	58.64	8.59	2.3	Between Groups	619.8	2	309.9	6.75	0.002
	Average	28	59.75	6.61	1.25	Within Groups	2478.86	54	45.91		
	Low	15	66.8	4.93	1.27	Total	3098.67	56			
	Total	57	61.33	7.44	0.99						
Attitude towards Teaching	High	16	17	2.28	0.57	Between Groups	176.7	2	88.35	7.78	0.001
	Average	32	17.75	3.89	0.69	Within Groups	715.78	63	11.36		
	Low	18	21.11	3.16	0.74	Total	892.49	65			
	Total	66	18.49	3.7	0.46						
Perceived Pro-fessionalism of Teaching	High	14	24.43	4.33	1.16	Between Groups	413.46	2	206.73	12.14	0
	Average	26	25.77	4.56	0.89	Within Groups	885.38	52	17.03		
	Low	15	31.33	2.94	0.76	Total	1298.84	54			
	Total	55	26.95	4.9	0.66						

Table 13.2 shows that there is no significant relationship between teacher trainees' level of agreement that teaching is a stereotyped career and motivation to achieve, attitude towards training programme, value attached to their training programme, and perceived effectiveness of teacher training programme (sig. > .05 hence the decision to retain the respective null hypotheses). However, significant relationship was established between the teacher trainees' level of agreement that teaching is a stereotyped career and attitude towards teaching, professionalism of teaching and willingness to teach (sig. < .05, hence the decision to reject the respective null hypotheses). Table 13.3 indicates that the teacher trainees with "low" level of stereotype were significantly more willing to teach, have favourable attitudes towards teaching and see teaching as a profession than those with "high" and "average" levels of stereotype.

Table 13.3: Post Hoc Analysis of Teacher Trainees' Perception of Teaching and Attitude towards Teacher Training Programme and Teaching

Dependent Variable	(I) Level to Which Teaching is Stereotyped	(J) Level to Which Teaching is Stereotyped	Mean Difference (I-J)	Std. Error	Sig.
Willingness to Teach	High	Average	-1.10714	2.21774	.620
		Low	-8.15714*	2.51779	.002
	Average	High	1.10714	2.21774	.620
		Low	-7.05000*	2.16790	.002
	Low	High	8.15714*	2.51779	.002
		Average	7.05000*	2.16790	.002
Attitude towards Teaching	High	Average	-.75000	1.03206	.470
		Low	-4.11111*	1.15814	.001
	Average	High	.75000	1.03206	.470
		Low	-3.36111*	.99310	.001
	Low	High	4.11111*	1.15814	.001
		Average	3.36111*	.99310	.001

		(Continued)			
Professionalism of Teaching	High	Average	-1.34066	1.36786	.332
		Low	-6.90476*	1.53339	.000
	Average	High	1.34066	1.36786	.332
		Low	-5.56410*	1.33790	.000
	Low	High	6.90476*	1.53339	.000
		Average	5.56410*	1.33790	.000

Discussion

University of Botswana teacher trainees felt that the career into which they are being trained is stereotyped as an inferior profession. This is in consonance with Nenty (2010). Such views ostracise teachers to the inferior end of the professional continuum. The belief that the society which they are serving views their occupation as an inferior career is a 'psychological threat' that haunts teachers in Botswana. As indicated before, such a threat inhibits behaviour desirable for achievement by teachers and hence by learners, and this in turn hurts the society. Such perception by the society is a disservice to a group of people who are rendering an indispensable service to her. The findings reveal that the level to which teaching is stereotyped relates negatively with willingness to teach, attitude towards teaching and value attached to the profession of teaching.

The dependent variables have positive inter-relationships and attitude showed the weakest relationship. The hypothesis tested revealed no significant relationship between the level to which teaching in stereotyped and attitude towards teaching, value of teacher training and effectiveness of teacher training program. The attitude of teachers towards their profession has always been found to relate significantly to teachers' behaviour and students' achievement. Milner and Hoy (2003) stated that teachers with favourable attitude are more open to new ideas and are creative. This finding, considered along with the theory of stereotype threat, implies that teachers with a feeling of high stereotype threat shy away from their profession and lack enthusiasm for the career. This is in concurrence with Ayodele and Adeyoju (1995) who explain that performance on a task is usually congruent with the attitude the person holds towards the task.

Many factors have been documented to be causing the negative stereotyping of the teaching profession. Historically, teaching changed from being men-dominated to women-dominated. Since society has culturally viewed women as a weaker gender, teaching, which tended to be viewed as 'a women's occupation', was belittled. This view rhymes with Dodeen, Ibrahim and Emad (2003) who report that attitude towards the teaching profession is influenced by gender, with female teachers having a more positive attitude than their male counterparts. Maliki (2013) found that low wages, low social value and lack of recognition reinforce stereotype threat among teachers. Psychological deprivation of teaching environments and stereotype threat emanating from society's view of the teaching profession contribute to alienation of teacher trainees.

Teacher trainees who saw teaching as highly stereotyped differed significantly from those who saw it as drawing low levels of stereotype in attitude towards the teaching profession. Similarly, Nenty (2010) revealed that the higher the level of stereotype threat the less favourable the teacher trainees' attitude towards their training programme. The higher the stereotype threat the poorer the attitude towards teaching. Moreover, based on several similar observations, Maliki (2013) also explained that stereotype threat may interrupt learning during teacher training. In the same way, Norris (2014) explains that academic performance can be harmed by awareness that one's behaviour might be viewed through the lens of career stereotype. To Norris, stereotype threat goes beyond underachievement in schools; it leads to loss in sense of belonging, reduced practice time for a task, and reduction in the value attached to the training programme. The present study corroborated these views.

Conclusion

A choice made to enter the teaching profession should be like a choice to enter any other profession. However, due to the inferior position society has given to teaching, capable students shun teacher training programmes. Over time, teaching has metamorphosed greatly in terms of motivation, qualification and structure. Some of these changes have dissuaded many people from choosing careers in teaching. Thus, reduction of stereotype threat on pre-service teachers might go a long way towards enabling realisation of the dream that the careers of teachers and the processes of teacher education are treated as a worthy continuum of professional growth.

References

Action Aid International Uganda, Development Research and Training, Uganda, National NGO Forum (2012). *Lost opportunity? Gaps in youth policy and programming in Uganda.* [Online]. Retrieved on April 10, 2014 from http://www.actionaid.org/sites/files/actionaid/youthrepot-final_0.pdf.

Ahimbisibwe, P. (2012, November 26). "42 KIU PhDs hang in balance". In *Daily Monitor,* p.1.

Ahmad, N., & Oranye, N.O. (2010). "Empowerment, job satisfaction and organizational commitment: A comparative analysis of nurses working in Malaysia and England". In *Journal of Nursing Management,* 18 (5): 582–91.

Allen, N. (2003). "Organizational commitment in the military: A discussion of theory and practice". In *Military Psychology,* 15: 237–253.

Allen, N.J., & Meyer, J. P. (1990). "The measurement and antecedents of affective, continuance and normative commitment to the organization". In *Journal of Occupational Psychology,* 63: 1–18.

Altbach, P.G. (2002). *The decline of the guru: The academic profession in developing and middle-income countries.* Chestnut Hill MA: Centre for International Higher Education, Boston College.

— (2005). "Universities family style". In *International Higher Education.* Number 39, 10–12.

— (2005a) "Contradictions of academic development: Exploiting the professoriate and weakening the university". In *International Higher Education.* Number 39, 2–3.

— (2006). *Comparative higher education: Knowledge, the university and development.* Boston, MA: Boston College Centre for International Higher Education.

Altbach, P.G., & Knight, J. (2007). "The internationalization of higher education: Motivations and realities". In *Journal of Studies in International Education,* 11 (3): 290–305.

Ambady, N., Shih, M., Kim, A., & Pittinsky, T.L. (2001). "Stereotype susceptibility in children: Effects of identity activation on quantitative performance". In *Psychological Science,* 12 (5): 385–390.

Amidon, D.M., Piero, F., & Mercier-Laurent, E. (Eds.). (2005). *Knowledge Economics: Principles, practices and policies.* London: Tartu University Press.

Amin, E.M. (2005). *Social science research: Conception, methodology and analysis.* Kampala: Makerere University Printery.

Amutabi, M.N. (2002). "Crisis and student protest in universities in Kenya: Examining the role of students in national leadership and the democratization process". In *African Studies Review,* 45 (2): 157–177.

Antón, C. (2009). "The impact of role stress on workers' behaviour through job satisfaction and organizational commitment". In *International Journal of Psychology,* 44 (3): 187–194.

Antràs, P., Garicano, L., & Rossi-Hansberg, E. (2006). "Offshoring in a knowledge economy". In *Quarterly Journal of Economics,* 121 (1): 31–77.

Askling, B. (2001). "Higher education and academic staff in a period of policy and system change". In *Higher Education* 41 (1-2): 157–181.

Assem, S., Dima, J., & Sarah, N. (2007). "Corporate governance and intellectual capital: Evidence from an academic institution". In *Corporate Governance* 9 (2): 146–157.

Aurangzeb, A., & Khola, A. (2012). "Developing good governance, management and leadership in universities and degree awarding institutions: A case of Pakistan". *International Journal of Academic Research in Business and Social Sciences,* 2 (11): 190–202.

Ayodele, S.O., & Adeyoju, C.A. (1995). "A study of Nigerian teachers' attitude towards the teaching profession". In *Nigeria Journal of Education Research,* 2 (1): 8–17.

Azmi, S. (2006). "Attaining and maintaining world class university standards". Paper presented at The Star/Asian Centre for Media Studies Conference 2006.

Bagraim, M. (2013). *Politicians driven by self-interest, not public service*. [Online]. Retrieved on April 13, 2014 from http://www.iol.co.za/business/opinion/letters/politicians-driven-by-self-interest-not-public-service-1.1587790#.U0pQ26KJOC4.

Bakia, M. (2002). "The cost components of computers in classrooms: Data from developing countries". In *TechKnowLogia*, January–March, 63–68.

Balfour, D., & Wechsler, B. (1996). "Organisational commitment: Antecedents and outcomes in public organisations". In *Public Productivity and Management Review*, 29: 256–277.

Bameka, P. (1996). "Factors affecting academic staff productivity at Makerere University". Unpublished Master's dissertation. Kampala: Makerere University.

Bamiro, O.A. (2012). "Transformation, reformation and challenges of higher education in Africa". Keynote address at the Seventh Regional Higher Education Research and Policy Network (HERPNET) Conference held at University of Ibadan Conference Centre (17 to 20 September, 2012).

Barrett, M. J., & Beaver, W. H. (1991). "American accounting association committee on accounting and auditing measurement, 1989–90". In *Accounting Horizons*, 5(3): 81–105.

Barten, P. E. (2006). *High school reform and work: facing labour market realities*. Princeton: Educational Testing Service.

Bartram, B. (2007). "The socio-cultural needs of international students in higher education: A comparison of staff and student views". *Journal of Studies in International Education*, 11 (2): 205–214.

Baumeister, R., & Leary, M. (1995). "The need to belong: Desire for interpersonal attachments as a fundamental human motivation". In *Psychological Bulletin*, 117(3): 497–529

Baumeister, R.F., & Kathleen, D.V. (2007). *Encyclopaedia of social psychology*. [Online]. Retrieved on April 13, 2014 from http://knowledge.sagepub.com/view/socialpsychology/n411.xml.

Becker, G.S. (1964). *Human Capital.* New York: Columbia University Press.

Beckmann, A., & Cooper, C. (2004). "Globalisation, the new managerialism and education: Rethinking the purpose of education in Britain". In *Journal for Critical Education Policy Studies*, 2 (2). [Online]. Retrieved on January 15, 2017 from http://sys.glotta.ntua.gr/Dialogos/Politics/NewManagerialismAndEducation.html.)

Beckmann, A., Cooper, C., & Hill, D. (2009). "Neoliberalisation and managerialisation of education in England and Wales: A case for reconstructing education". In *Journal for Critical Education Policy Studies*, 7(2): 311–345.

Bengson, J., & Moffett, M.A. (Eds.). (2011). *Essays on knowledge, mind, and action.* New York: Oxford University Press.

Bhargava, A., & Pathy, M. (2014). "Attitude of student teachers towards teaching profession". *Turkish Online Journal of Distance Education*, 15 (3): 26–36.

Bisaso, R. (2006). "Optimizing the potential of educational computing research in emerging countries". In V. Baryamureeba & W. Ddembe (Eds.). *Measuring computing research excellence and vitality* (pp. 56–62). Kampala: Fountain Publishers.

Black, W. K. (2005). *The best way to rob a bank is to own one: how corporate executives and politicians looted the S&L industry.* Texas: University of Texas Press.

Bleiklie, I., & Kogan, M. (2007). "Organisation and governance of universities". In *Higher Education Policy*, 20 (4): 477–493.

Bolaji, S. D. (2011). "Dewey's philosophy and contemporary education in Nigeria: Implication for democracy and education". Unpublished PhD thesis. Lagos: University of Lagos-Akoka.

Bontis, N. (1996). "There's a price on your head: Managing intellectual capital strategically". In *Business Quarterly*, 60 (4): 40–47.

— (1998). "Intellectual capital: An exploratory study that develops measures and models". In *Management Decision*, 36 (2): 63–76.

Bontis, N., & Serenko, A. (2007). "The moderating role of human capital management practices on employee capabilities". In *Journal of Knowledge Management*, 11(3): 31–51.

Booth, W.C., Colomb, G.G., & Williams, J.M. (2008). *The craft of research* (3rd Ed). Chicago: The University of Chicago Press.

Borden, V.M.H., & Owens, J.L.Z. (2001). *Measuring quality: Choosing among surveys and other assessments of college quality.* Washington, DC: Association for Institutional Research for Management Research, Policy Analysis and Planning.

Bradley, K. (1997). Intellectual capital and the new wealth of nations. *Business Strategy Review*, 8 (1): 53–62.

Brailsford, I. (2010). "Motives and aspirations for doctoral study: Career, personal and inter-personal factors in the decision to embark on a history PhD". In *International Journal of Doctoral Studies*, 5: 15–27.

Brianna, M. S., & Ashleigh, F.B. (2013). "Examining the domain-specificity of metacognition using academic domains and task-specific individual differences". In *Australian Journal of Educational and Developmental Psychology*, 13: 28–43.

Brooks, R. & Waters, J. (2009a), "A second chance at "success": UK students and global circuits of higher education", In *Sociology*, 43: 1085–1102.

— (2009b). "International higher education and the mobility of UK students". In *Journal of Research in International Education,* 8(2): 191–209.

Buchere, D. (2009, February 8). "East Africa: New quality assurance system". In *University World News,* Issue No. 22.

Burson, K.A., Larrick, R.P., & Klayman, J. (2006). "Skilled or unskilled, but still unaware of it: How perceptions of difficulty drive miscalibration in relative comparisons". In *Journal of Personality and Social Psychology,* 90(1): 60–77.

Businge, C. & Karugaba, M. (2012, April 16). "Staff shortage crippling universities". In *The New Vision,* p.1.

Byrne, M., & Flood, B. (2005). "A study of accounting students' motives, expectations and preparedness for higher education". In *Journal of Further and Higher Education,* 29(2): 111–124.

Callan, P., & Immerwahr, J. (2008). What colleges must do to keep the public's good will. *Chronicle of Higher Education*. [Online]. Retrieved on January 16, 2017 from http://www.csun.edu/pubrels/clips/Jan08/01-07-08R.pdf.

Camilleri, E. (2002). Some antecedents of organisational commitment: results from an information systems public sector organization. *Bank of Valletta Review*, No. 2, 1–29.

Cavell, S. (2002). *Knowing and acknowledging: Must we mean what we say?* Cambridge: Cambridge University Press.

Cetin, M.O. (2006). "The relationship between job satisfaction, occupational, and organizational commitment of academics". In *The Journal of the American Academy of Business*, 8 (1): 78–88.

Chan, R., Brown, G. T., & Ludlow, L. (2014). *What is the purpose of higher education? A comparison of institutional and student perspectives on the goals and purposes of completing a bachelor's degree in the 21st century*. [Online]. Retrieved on February 22, 2014 from http://www.academia.edu/2626994/What_is_the_purpose_of_higher_education_Comparing_student_and_institutional_perspectives_for_completing_a_bachelors_degree_in_the_21st_century.

Chang, H., Chi, N., & Miao, M. (2007). "Testing the relationship between three-component organizational/occupational commitment and organizational/occupational turnover intention using a non-recursive model. In *Journal of Vocational Behaviour*, 70 (2): 352–368.

Chetro-Szivos, J. (2010). Cross-border tertiary education: Challenges and opportunities for intercultural understanding. In *Journal of Intercultural Management*, 2(1): 5–22.

CIEFFA/AUC (2009). *Implementing piority area one (gender and culture) of the AU second decade of education in Africa: 2006-2015 (A synthesis of four sub-regional surveys)*. Ouagadougou: CIEFFA/AUC.

CIPD (2001). *Employers' perceptions of the psychological contract.* CIPD Report 112.

Commission for Higher Education (CHE). (2008). *Handbook on process for quality assurance in higher education in Kenya.* Nairobi: *Commission for Higher Education.*

Cook, J., & Mansfield, R. (2013). *Task-specific experience and task-specific talent: Decomposing the productivity of high school teachers.* [Online]. Retrieved on April 12, 2014 from http://www.econ.queensu.ca/files/event/Cook-Mansfield_Task_Specific_Experience.pdf.

CoSN (2001). *Taking TCO to the classroom: a school administrator's guide to planning for the total cost of new technology.* Washington DC.: CoSN.

— (2003). *Why total cost of ownership (TCO) matters: A report and estimating tool for k-12 school districts.* Washington DC.: CoSN.

Court, D. (1999). *Financing higher education in Africa: Makerere, the quiet revolution.* Washington DC: Rockefeller Foundation and the World Bank.

Crandall, R.W. (2004). *Competition and chaos: US telecommunications since the 1996 Telecom Act.* Washington DC.: Brookings Institute Press.

Creswell, J.W. (2012). *Educational research: Planning, conducting, and evaluating quantitative and qualitative research.* Upper Saddle River, NJ: Prentice Hall.

Crossan, M.M., & Apaydin, M. (2010). "Multi-dimensional framework of organizational innovation: A systematic review of literature". *Journal of Management Studies,* 47 (6): 1154 –1191.

Crowther, G. (1969) Address at the formal inauguration of The Open University. [Online]. Retrieved on April 10, 2014 from: http://www.col.org/SiteCollectionDocuments/Daniel_CROWTHER_Speech_1969.pdf.

Dae-Bong, K. (2009). *Human capital and its measurement.* The 3rd OECD World Forum on Statistics, Knowledge and Policy: Charting Progress, Building Visions, Improving Life, Busan, Korea 27–30 October. [Online]. Retrieved on April 11, 2014 from http://www.oecd.org/site/progresskorea/44111355.pdf.

Danby, S. J., & McWilliam, E. (2005). "Respecting and challenging the candidate: some developments in program design". In Maxwell, T.W., Hickey, C. & Evans, T. (Eds.) *Proceedings Fifth International Professional Doctorates Conference: 'Working doctorates: the impact of professional doctorates in the professions',* pp. 1–46, Geelong, Victoria: Deakin University.

D'Antoni, S. (2009). "Open Educational Resources: Reviewing initiatives and issues". In *Open Learning, The Journal of Open, Distance and e-Learning.* 24 (1): 3–10.

Davies, B., Gottsche, M., & Bansel, P. (2006). "The rise and fall of the neoliberal university". In *European Journal of Education,* 41(2): 305–319.

Davila, M.C. & Garcia, G.J. (2012). "Organizational identification and commitment: Correlates of senses of belonging and affective commitment". In *The Spanish Journal of Psychology,* 15 (1): 244–255.

Delanty, G. (2003). "Ideologies of knowledge society and the cultural contradictions of higher education". In *Policy Futures in Education,* 1(1): 71–82.

Dello Russo, S., Vecchione, M. & Borgogni, L. (2013). "Commitment profiles, job satisfaction, and behavioural outcomes". In *Applied Psychology: An International Review,* 62 (4): 701–719.

DeRouin, R.E., Fritzsche, B.A., & Salas, E. (2003). "Stereotype threat and training performance". [Online]. Retrieved from https://www.psychologicalscience.org/cfs/program/view_submission.cfm?Abstract_ID=348.

Dill, D.D. (2001). "The 'Marketization' of higher education: Changes in Academic Competition and Implications for University Autonomy and Accountability", In *Higher Education Policy.* 14(1): 21–35.

Diouf, M. & Mamdani, M. (Eds.) (1994). *Academic Freedom in Africa.* Dakar: CODESRIA.

Dirani, K.M. & Kuchinke, K.P. (2011). "Job satisfaction and organizational commitment: Validating the Arabic satisfaction and commitment questionnaire (ASCQ), testing the correlations, and investigating the effects of demographic variables in the Lebanese banking sector". In *The International Journal of Human Resource Management,* 22 (5): 1180–1202.

Djeflat, A. (2009). *Building knowledge economies for job creation, increased competitiveness, and balanced development.* World Bank Draft. [Online]. Retrieved on April 11, 2014 from http://info.worldbank.org/etools/docs/library/252537/2009-12-18-142047_ADjeflat%20_Background_Report.pdf.

Dodeen, H. A., Ibrahim, A. A., & Emad, M. (2003). "Attitude of pre-service teachers towards persons with disabilities: Predictions for the success of inclusion". In *College Student Journal*, 37(4): 515–521.

Døving, E., & Nordhaug, O. (2002). "Learning firm specific knowledge and skills: Conceptual issues and empirical results". Paper presented to OKLC 2002 (academic track). *The 3rd European Conference on Organizational Knowledge, Learning and Capabilities*. Athens, April 5th - 6th. [Online]. Retrieved on April 12, 2014 from http://www2.warwick.ac.uk/fac/soc/wbs/conf/olkc/archive/oklc3/papers/id341.pdf.

Drucker, P. & Hodge, C. (2000). *Post-Capitalist Society*. New York: HarperCollins Publishers, Inc.

Dunham, R., Grube, J., & Castaneda, M. (1994). "Organisational commitment: The utility of an integrative definition". In *Journal of Applied Psychology*, 79(3): 370–380.

Dutta, S. (Ed). (2012). *The global innovation index 2012: Stronger innovation linkages for global growth*. [Online]. Retrieved on April 11, 2014 from http://www.wipo.int/export/sites/www/freepublications/en/economics/gii/gii_2012.pdf.

Eddy, M.D. (2013). "The shape of knowledge: Children and the visual culture of literacy and numeracy". In *Science in Context*, 26(2): 215–245.

EPRC (1989). *Education for national integration and development*. Kampala: Ministry of Education.

Enders, J. (2001). "A chair system in transition: Appointments, promotions and gate-keeping in German". *Higher Education* 41(3): 3–25.

Erbas, M.K. (2014). "The relationship between alienation levels of physical education teacher candidates and their attitudes towards the teaching profession." In *Australian Journal of Teacher Education*, 39 (8): 37–52.

FDRE (2009). *Higher Education Proclamation No. 650/2009*. Federal Negarit Gazeta of the Democratic Republic of Ethiopia. Addis Ababa: Author.

Field, A. P. (2005). *Discovering statistics using SPSS* (2nd Edition). London: Sage.

Fielden, J. (2008). "Global trends in university governance". Working paper series number 9. Washington DC: World Bank.

Finch, J. (1995). *Quality and its measurement: A business perspective*. Great Britain: The Society for Research into Higher Education.

Freedberg, L. (2013, September 24). *Enrollment in teacher preparation programs plummets*. Oakland: Edsource.

Fridoon, J. & Nasrin, S. (2009). "Three components of organizational commitment and job satisfaction of hospital nurses in Iran". In *The Health Care Manager*, 28: 375–380.

Furnham, A., Christopher, A.N., Garwood, J., & Neil, M.G. (2007). "Approaches to learning and the acquisition of general knowledge". In *Personality and Individual Differences*, 43 (6): 1563–1571.

Gaidzanwa, R. (1994). *Governance issues in African universities: Improving management and governance to make African universities viable in the 1990s and beyond*. Accra: Working Group on Higher Education.

Gardner, J.W. (1961). *Excellence: Can we be equal and excellent?* New York: Harper and Brothers.

Gebru, D.A. (2014). "Graduate Preparation in Ethiopian Public Higher Education Institutions: Perceptions of Academic Staff". In Paschal B. Mihyo (Ed.). *Employment Policies and Unemployment in Eastern and Southern Africa*. Addis Ababa: Organization for Social Science Research in Eastern and Southern Africa.

Gilroy, P., Long, P., Rangecroft, M., & Tricker, T. (1999). "The evaluation of course quality through a service template". In *Evaluation*, 5(1): 80–91.

Giroux, H. (2003). "Selling out higher education". In *Policy Futures in Education*, 1(1): 179–200.

Goe, L. (2007). *The link between quality of teaching and student outcomes: A research synthesis*. Washington DC: National Comprehensive Centre for Quality of teaching.

Goodlad, S. (1995). *The quest for quality: Sixteen forms of heresy in higher education*. Great Britain: The Society for Research into Higher Education.

Gornitzka, A. (1999). "Governmental policies and organisational change in higher education". In *Higher Education,* 38(1): 5–31.

Gottschalk-Mazouz, N. (2008). "Internet and the flow of knowledge". In Hrachovec, H., Pichler, A. (Eds.). *Philosophy of the information society.* Cambridge: Cambridge University Press.

Green, D. (1995). *What is quality in higher education? Concepts, policy and practice.* Great Britain: The Society for Research into Higher Education.

Green, S., Anderson, S., & Shivers, S. (1996). "Demographics and organisational influences on leader-member exchange and related work attitudes". In *Organisational Behaviour and Human Decision Processes,* 66 (2): 203–214.

Griliches, Z. (1990). "Patent statistics are economic indicators: A survey". In *Journal of Economic Literature,* 10 (2): 1661–1707.

Gutierrez, A.P., Candel, L.L. & Carver, L. (2012). "The structural relationship between organizational commitment, global job satisfaction, development experience, work values, organizational support, and person-organizational fit among nursing faculty". In *Journal of Advanced Nursing,* 54: 1601–1614.

Habib, A., Morrow, S., & Bentley, K. (2008). "Academic freedom, institutional autonomy and the corporatised university in contemporary South Africa". In *Social Dynamics,* 34(2): 140–155.

Hall, K. (2005). "Science, globalisation and educational governance: The political rationalities of the new managerialism". *Indiana Journal of Global Legal Studies,* 12(1): 153–182.

Hanushek, E.A., Kain, J.F., O'Brien, D.M., & Rivkin S.G. (2005). *The market for quality of teaching.* Cambridge: National Bureau of Economic Research.

Hayward, F. M. (2006). "Quality assurance and accreditation of higher education in Africa". Paper presented at the Conference on Higher Education Reform in Francophone Africa held at Ouagadougou, Burkina Faso, in June 2006.

Hayward, M. F., & Ncayiyana, D. J. (2006). *Report on the National Education Sector Plan Project:* Lilongwe: Ministry of Education and Vocational Training.

Honan, J., & Teferra, D. (2001). "The US academic profession: Key challenges". *Higher Education,* 41(1/2): 183–203.

Howey, K.R., & Gardner, W.E. (1983). *The education of teachers — a look ahead.* New York: Longman.

Hulpia, H., Devos, G., & Rosseel, Y. (2009). "The relationship between the perception of distributed leadership in secondary schools and teachers' and teacher leaders' job satisfaction and organizational commitment". In *School Effectiveness and School Improvement,* 20 (3): 291–317.

Ihme, T. A., & Moller, J. (2015). "'He who can, does; he who cannot, teaches?': Stereotype threat and preservice teachers". *Journal of Educational Psychology,* 107 (1): 300-308.

International Association of Universities, Association of Universities and Colleges of Canada, American Council on Education & Council for Higher Education Accreditation (2005). "Sharing Quality Higher Education Across Borders: A Statement on Behalf of Higher Education Institutions Worldwide". In *International Higher Education.* Number 39, 3–6.

Ishengoma, J.M. (2003). *The myths and realities of higher education globalization: a view from the Southern Hemisphere.* [Online]. Retrieved December 23, 2013 from http://escotet.org/in-focus/openforum/the-myths-and-realities-of-higher-education-globalization-a-viewfrom-the-southern-hemisphere.

Inter-University Council for East Africa (2009). *A study on the harmonization of the East African education systems.* Kampala: Author.

Jackson, R. S., Davis, J. H. & Jackson, F. R. (2010). "Redesigning regional accreditation: The impact on institutional planning". In *Planning for Higher Education,* 38 (4): 9–19.

Jackson, T.A., Meyer, J. P. & Wang, X.H. (2013). "Leadership, commitment, and culture: A meta-analysis". In *Journal of Leadership and Organizational Studies,* 20 (1): 84–106.

Jaramogi, P. (2013). "Kyambogo varsity staff demand 300% pay-rise". [Online]. Retrieved on December 17, 2014 from http://www.newvision.co.ug/mobile/detail.aspx?newsid=19051&catid=6.

Jaros, S. (2007). "Meyer and Allen model of organizational commitment: Measurement issues". In *The Icfai Journal of Organizational Behaviour*, 7(4): 7-25.

Kagolo, F. (2013). "Makerere lecturers call off strike". [Online]. Retrieved on December 17, 2014 from http://www.newvision.co.ug/news/646659-makerere-lecturers-call-off-strike.html.

Kanning, U.P., & Hill, A. (2014). "Validation of the organizational commitment questionnaire (OCQ)". [Online]. Retrieved on December 17, 2014 from http://journal-bmp.de/2013/12/validation-of-the-organizational-commitment-questionnaire-ocq-in-six-languages/?lang=en.

Kasenene, E. S. (2009). "Are African universities centres of excellence? The consumer perspective of Ugandan universities". In *Makerere Journal of Higher Education*, 2: 80-94.

Kasozi, A.B.K. (2003). *University education in Uganda: Challenges and opportunities for reform*. Kampala: Fountain Publishers. Kassam, A. (1999). University education in Uganda: Quality despite adversity. *The UNESCO Courier*, Number 173, 11–25.

— (2009). "The plight and failures of the academic staff in public universities". [Online]. Retrieved on February 10, 2017 from http://ahero.uwc.ac.za/index.php?module=cshe&action=downloadfile&fileid 36807145012409869563440.

Keenan, J., & Aggestam, M. (2001). "Corporate governance and intellectual capital: Some conceptualizations". In *Corporate Governance: An International Review*, 9(4): 259–275.

Kerr, D., & Mapanje, J. (2002). "Academic freedom and the University of Malawi". In *African Studies Review*, 45(2): 73–91.

Knight, J. (2006). *Higher education crossing borders: A guide to the implications of the General Agreements on Trade in Services (GATS) for cross-border education*. Vancouver, Commonwealth of Learning.

— (2007). *Cross-border tertiary education: A way towards capacity development*. Vancouver, World Bank & OECD.

Krejcie, R. V., & Morgan, D. W. (1970). "Determining sample size for research activities" In *Educational and Psychological Measurement*, 30

(3): 607-610. Krishna, K. (1996). *Library manual.* New Delhi: Vikas Publishing House.

Kulwinder, S. (2011). "Study of achievement motivation in relation to academic achievement of students". In *International Journal of Educational Planning & Administration*, 1(2): 161–171.

Kwesiga J., & Ahikire, J. (2006). "On student access and equity in a reforming university: Makerere in the 1990s and beyond". In *Journal of Higher Education in Africa*, 4(2): 1–46.

Lent, R.W., & Brown, S.D. (2006). "On conceptualizing and assessing social cognitive constructs in career research: A measurement guide". In *Journal of Career Assessment*, 14 (1): 12–35.

Lewin, K. M. (2007). "Improving access, transition and equity: Creating a research agenda". *CREATE pathway to success monograph series*. Number 1. University of Sussex Centre for International Education.

Lipset, S.M. (1959). "Some social requisites of democracy: Economic development and political legitimacy". In *American political science review.* 53(1): 69–105.

Liu, J. (2010). "The changing body of students: A study of the motives, expectations and preparedness of postgraduate marketing students". In *Marketing Intelligence and Planning* 28 (7): 812–830.

Loing, B. (2005). "ICT and higher education: 9th UNESCO/NGO higher education collective consultation on higher education". [Online]. Retrieved on January 22, 2017 from http://www.unesco.org/ngo/comite/cpmother/enseign-sup/tic-gb.pdf.

Lule, J.A. (2013). "62% of Ugandan youth are jobless". [Online]. Retrieved on April 10, 2014 from http://www.newvision.co.ug/news/639446-62-of-ugandan-youth-jobless--report.html.

Lynch, K. (2006). "Neo-liberalism and marketisation: The implications for higher education". In *European Educational Research Journal*. 5(1): 1–17.

Major, E., T., & Tiro, L. (2012). "Theory vs. practice: The case of primary teacher education in Botswana". In *International Journal of Scientific Research in Education*, 5: 63-70.

Malawi Government (2000). *Policy and Investment Framework (PIF) 2000–2015*. Lilongwe: Author.

— (2006). *National Education Sector Plan*. Lilongwe: Author.

Maliki, A.E. (2013). "Attitudes towards the teaching profession of students from the faculty of education, Niger Delta University". In *International Journal of Social Sciences*, 1, 11–18.

Mamdani, M. (2007). *Scholars in the marketplace: The dilemmas of neo-liberal reform at Makerere University, 1989–2005*. Kampala: Fountain Publishers.

Mann, G.A. (2013). "A motive to serve: Public service motivation in human resource management and the role of PSM in the non-profit sector". In *Public Personnel Management*, 35(1): 33–48.

Marginson, S. (2002). "Nation-building universities in a global environment: The case of Australia". *Higher Education*, 43(3): 409–428.

Massy, W. (2011). "Objectives and success measures for higher education". [Online]. Retrieved on April 10, 2014 from http://net.educause.edu/ir/library/pdf/ff0910s.pdf.

Materu, P. (2007). "Higher education quality assurance in sub-Saharan Africa: Status, challenges, opportunities and promising practices." (Working Paper No. 124). Washington, DC: World Bank.

Mayanja, M. K. (1996). *The social background of Makerere University students and the potential for cost sharing*. Accra: Association of African Universities.

— (2007). "Improving income from internally generated funds without provoking students or staff strikes at Makerere and other universities". In *Uganda Higher Education Review*. 4(2): 2–8.

Mazzarol, T., & Soutar, G.N. (2002). "Push-pull factors influencing international student destination choice". In *International Journal of Education Management*, 16(2): 82–90.

McGregor, G. P. (2007). *King's College Budo: Centenary history, 1906-2006*. Kampala: Fountain Publishers.

McMahon, B. (2009). "Organizational commitment, relationship commitment and their association with attachment style and locus of control". [Online]. Retrieved on December

19, 2014 from https://smartech.gatech.edu/bitstream/handle/1853/14502/mcmahon_brian_200705_mast.pdf;jsessionid=56110740790EAAFA92B92E99A057B528.smart2?sequence=1.

Meyer, J.P. & Allen, N.J. (1997). *Commitment in the workplace: Theory, research and application*. Thousand Oaks, CA: Sage.

Meyer, J.P., Stanley, D. J., Jackson, T. A., McInnis, K.J., Maltin, E.R. & Sheppard, L. (2012). "Affective, normative, and continuance commitment levels across cultures: A meta-analysis". In *Journal of Vocational Behaviour*, 80 (1): 225–245.

Meyer, J.P., Srinivas, E.S., Lal, J.B., & Topolnytsky, L. (2007). "Employee commitment and support for an organizational change: Test of the three-component model in two cultures". In *Journal of Occupational and Organizational Psychology*, 80 (2): 185–211.

Mguqulwa, N. (2008). "The relationship between organisational commitment and work performance in an agricultural company". [Online]. Retrieved on December 17, 2014 from http://uir.unisa.ac.za/bitstream/handle/10500/2401/dissertation.pdf?sequence=1THE.

Middlehurst, R., & Campbell, C. (2003). *Quality assurance and borderless higher education: Finding pathways through the maze*. [Online]. Retrieved on February 10, 2017 from https://www.google.co.ugurl?sa=t&rct=j&q=&esrc=s&source=web&cd=1&ved=IAXsQFggzMAA&url=http%3A%2F%2Fwww.obhe.ac.uk2Fdocuments%2F2003%2FReports2FQuality_Assurance_and_Borderless_Higher_Education_Finding_Pathways_through_the_Maze&usg=AFQjCNHKULAfpcGt2aJCZ4HbnYRP5wEWNg&sig23hHEnmrd41OITWj0dm9LGQ&bvm=bv.146496531,d.d24&cad=rja.

Mignerey, J., Rubin, R., & Gordon, W. (1995). "Organisational entry: An investigation of newcomer communication behaviour and uncertainty". In *Communication Research*, 22: 54–85.

Mills, L.R. (2009). "Applying social cognitive career theory to college science majors". [Online]. Retrieved from http://lib.dr.iastate.edu/cgi/viewcontent.cgi?article=1687&context=etd.

Milner, H. R., & Hoy, W. A. (2003). "Teacher self-efficacy and retaining talented teachers: A case study of an African-American teacher". In *Teaching and Teacher Education,* 19: 263–276.

Ministry of Education. (2003). *The eighth review of the Ministry of Education,* Kampala: Author.

Moja, T., Muller, J., & Cloete, N. (1996). "Towards new forms of regulation in higher education: The case of South Africa". In *Higher Education,* 32 (2): 129–155.

Monash University (2001). *Quality at Monash: Values and Principles.* Monash: Centre for Higher Education Quality.

Moore, M. G., & Lambert, K. I. (1996). "Motives for collaborating in international higher distance education". [Online]. Retrieved December 20, 2016 from http://www.cde.psu.edu/DE/ACSDE/ACSD.htm.

Mugizi, W. (2007). "Motivation and work attitude of academic staff in public universities in Uganda: A Case of Mbarara University of Science and Technology". Makerere University: Unpublished M. Ed. Dissertation. [Online]. Retrieved on September 17, 2013 from http://hdl.handle.net/10570/958.

Mulindwa, D. K. (1998). "ITEK years: Kyambogo since 1985". In C. B. Adupa, & D. K. Mulindwa (Eds.), *Institute of Teacher Education Kyambogo* (pp. 130–166). Kampala: ITEK.

Mullins, L. J. (2010). *Management and organizational behaviour.* London: Pitman.

Mushi, H.K., & Muganda, C. K. (2011). "Open Education Resources for National Development in Tanzania". Paper presented at the National ODL Conference, Arusha, 10th – 11th May 2011.

Mutum, R. (2007). "Attitude of pre-service student-teacher of CTE (B.Ed. Course) towards teaching profession". [Online]. Retrieved November 3, 2008, from www.Academia.edu/6519875/attitude-of-preservice-student-teacher.

Mwesigwa, A. (2014). "Uganda's unemployed graduates held back by skills gap". [Online]. Retrieved on April 10, 2014 from http://www.theguardian.com/global-development/2014/jan/16/uganda-unemployed-graduates-held-back-skills-gap.

Mzuzu University. (1997). *Mzuzu University Act*. Mzuzu: Author.

Nabayego, C. (2011). *Adoption of informal education practices in management of formal education in central Uganda*. Makerere University: Unpublished PhD thesis.

Nabulya, R. (2013). "Youth unemployment rate hits 80%". [Online]. Retrieved on April 10, 2014 from http://chimpreports.com/index.php/special-reports/14509-youth-unemployment-rate-hits-80.html.

Nakanyike, B. M., & Nansozi, K. M. (2003). *Makerere University in transition (1993–2000): Opportunities and challenges*. Oxford: James Currey.

Nakyondwa, J. (2007, January 7). "Polof Senteza: Ddereeva w'eby'Enjigiriza mu Uganda" (Prof Senteza: Driver of Education in Uganda). In *Bukedde ku Ssande*, p.18.

Nanoka, I., & Takeuchi, H. (1995). *The knowledge-creating company*. New York: Oxford University Press.

National Council for Law Reporting. (2012). "Laws of Kenya: Universities act chapter 210B". Nairobi: Author.

NCHE (2004). *Checklist of quality and institution capacity indicators for assessment of institutions and programs under the UOTIA, 2001, Rules and Regulations No. 7*. Kampala: NCHE.

— (2006). *The state of higher education and training in Uganda 2006: A report on higher education delivery and institutions*. Kampala: Author.

— (2006b). *Graduate tracer and employers' expectations in Uganda*. Kampala: Author.

— (2010). *The state of higher education and training in Uganda 2010: A report on higher education delivery and institutions*. Kampala: Author

Nelson, R., & Phelps, E. (1966). "Investment in humans, technological diffusion and economic growth". In *American Economic Review*, 51 (2): 69–75.

Nenty, H. J., Moyo, S., & Phuti, F. (2015). "Perception of teaching as a profession and UB teacher trainees' attitude towards training programme and teaching". Paper presented during 4th International conference on Education, Kenyatta University, July 14–16, 2015.

Nenty, J., H. 2010. "Threat of perceived stereotype on behaviour related to choice of and practices in teaching as a career among teacher trainees". In *International Journal of Scientific Research in Education*, 3(2): 82–93

Nicolescu, L. (2005). "Private versus public in Romania: Consequences for the market". In *International Higher Education*. Number 39, Spring (2005). [Online]. Retrieved February 5, 2017 from http://ejournals.bc.edu/ojs/index.php/ihe/article/view/7477.

Njuguna, F.W. & Itegi, F. M. (2013). "Cross-border higher education in Africa: The Kenyan experience". *Journal of Emerging Trends in Educational Research and Policy Studies*, 4 (5): 752–759.

Nkunya, M.H.H. (2008). "Overview of higher education quality assurance system in East Africa". [Online]. Retrieved on February 5, 2017 from http://www.afriqunits.org/public_documents/2-IUCEAEdulinkOct08.pdf.

Norris, A. 2014. "What is stereotype threat?" [Online]. Retrieved on February 5, 2017 from http://www.reducingstereotypethreat.org/definition.html.

Ntambaazi, W.G. (2013). "View point: 83% youth unemployment is a time bomb!" [Online]. Retrieved on April 10, 2014 from http://www.observer.ug/index.php?option=com_content&view=article&id=19358:view-point-83-youth-unemployment-is-a-time-bomb.

Nunan, T. (July 1999). "Graduate qualities, employment and mass higher education". HERDSA Annual International Conference, Melbourne, 12-15 July 1999, Flexible Learning Centre, University of South Australia.

O'Malley, M. (2000). *Creating commitment*. London: John Wiley & Sons.

OECD (2001). *OECD Principles of Corporate Governance*. Paris: OECD.

— (2004). *Quality and recognition in higher education: The cross-border challenge*. Paris: OECD.

— (2007). *Giving knowledge for free: The emergence of open educational resources*. Paris: OECD Publishing.

— (2008). *Tertiary Education for the Knowledge Society.* Volume 1. Paris: OECD.

Ogidan, R., & Sanusi, J. (2011). "Role of the African Council for Distance Education in Fostering Quality Assurance in Open and Distance Learning in Africa". In *Makerere Journal of Higher Education,* 3(1): 101–115.

Ogom, R. O. (2007). "Tertiary education and development in sub-Saharan Africa at the dawn of the twenty first century: A lost hope, or present opportunity?". In *National Social Science Journal,* 29 (1): 108–120.

Oketch, M. (2004). "The emergence of private university education in Kenya: Trends, prospects, and challenges". In *International Journal of Education Development* 24 (2): 119–136.

Olsen, M., & Peters, M. (2005). "Neoliberalism, higher education and the knowledge economy: From the free market to knowledge capitalism". In *Journal of Education Policy,* 20(3): 313–345.

Olssen, M., Codd, J., & O'Neill, A.M. (2004). *Education policy: Globalisation, citizenship and democracy.* London: Sage.

Omari, I. M. (1991). *Higher education at crossroads in Africa.* Nairobi: Man Graphics Limited.

Ouma, P. N., Owoeye, J. S., & Oyebade, S. A. (2012). "Attractions to and challenges involved in studying abroad: The case of Kampala International University Students". In *Makerere Journal of Higher Education,* 3(2): 19–27.

Oyebade, S. A., & Keshinro, O. A. (2007). "The gap between the demand for and supply of university education in Nigeria (1979–2002)". In *Kampala International University Research Digest,* 1(1): 60-67.

PDD (2000). *Makerere University Strategic Plan 2000–2008.* Kampala: Makerere University Printery.

— (2008) *Makerere University Strategic Plan 2008–2018.* Kampala: Makerere University Printery.

Peltoniemi, M. (2006). *Diversity of the intellectual capital of firms within an industry.* Tampere: BRC Research Reports.

Peters, M. (2003). "Classical political economy and the role of universities in the new knowledge economy". In *Globalisation, Societies and Education,* 1: 153–168.

Posner, D. (1995). "Malawi's new dawn". In *Journal of Democracy,* 6(1):131–145.

Pritchard, D. (2007). "Recent work on epistemic value". In *American Philosophical Quarterly,* 44 (2): 85–110.

Radwan, I., & Pellegrini, G. (2010). *Knowledge, productivity, and innovation in Nigeria: Creating a new economy.* Washington, DC: The World Bank.

Ramirez, G. B. (2014). "Trading quality across borders: Colonial discourse and international quality assurance policies in higher education". In *Tertiary Education and Management,* 20 (2): 121–134.

Reed, M. I., Meek, & L., Jones, G. A. (2002). "Introduction". In A. Amaral, G.A. Jones, B. Karseth (Eds.) *Governing higher education: National perspectives on institutional governance.* Dordrecht/Boston/London: Kluwer Academic Publishers, pp. xv-xxxi.

Republic of Uganda. (2001). *UOTIA, 2001.* Entebbe: Uganda Printing and Publishing Corporation.

Robert N.J. (nd). "Expressing a good will: Kant on the motive of duty". [Online]. Retrieved on April 13, 2014 from http://web.missouri.edu/~johnsonrn/duty.html.

Rogers, E.M. (2003). *Diffusion of innovations* (5th ed.). New York: Free Press.

Rubadiri, J.D. (2002). "Educated African: Yet another song". Paper presented as Third Commencement Lecture of Nkumba University, April 10, 2002.

Ruwa, M. (2007). *Educational reform for what? Book of Reading Nigerian Philosophy of Education.* Jos: Saniez Books.

Saint, W. (1992). "Universities in Africa: strategies for stabilization and revitalization". World Bank Technical Paper, No. 194. Washington DC: The World Bank.

Saint, W. (2009). "Legal frameworks for higher education governance in sub-Saharan Africa". In *Higher Education Policy,* 22(4): 523–550.

Salmi, J. (2009a). *The Challenge of Establishing World-Class Universities*. Washington, DC: The World Bank.

— (2009b). "The growing accountability agenda in tertiary education: progress or mixed Blessing? Education working paper series No. 16. Washington, DC: The World Bank.

Samoff, J., & Carrol, B. (2003). "From manpower planning to the knowledge era: World Bank policies on higher education". UNESCO Occasional Paper Series. Paper Number 2. [Online]. Retrieved on February 6, 2017 from http://unesdoc.unesco.org/images/0013/001347/134782eo.pdf.

Sanchez, M.P., Elena, S., & Castrillo, R. (2006). "Intellectual capital management and reporting for universities: Usefulness, comparability and diffusion". [Online]. Retrieved on February 6, 2017 from www.ticinoricerca.ch/conference/abstracts/sanchez_abstract.pdf.

Sanga, P. L. (2012). "Case for a regional approach to the regulation of cross-border higher education with specific reference to East Africa". *Makerere Journal of Higher Education,* 4 (1): 45–59.

Sawyerr, A. (2004). "Challenges facing African universities: Selected issues". In *African Studies Review*, 47(1): 1–59.

Schultz, T.W. (1981). *Investing in people: The Economics of population quality*. Berkeley, CA: University of California Press.

Schwartz, S. (2003). "The higher purpose". [Online]. Retrieved on April 10, 2014 from http://www.timeshighereducation.co.uk/176727.article.

Scott, H. (2010). Defining power, motive. [Online]. Retrieved on April 13, 2014 from http://www.rationalskepticism.org/philosophy/definding-power-motive-t16816.html.

— (1997). "From elitist towards mass higher education: Phenomenon of private universities in Uganda". In *Uganda Education Journal,* 1, 23–30.

— (1999). "Management and leadership of a private university". In *Nkumba Business Journal, 1(1)*: 7–19.

— (2001). "Coping with the challenges of higher education in the 21st century". In W. M. Mande (Ed.), *Effective teaching in higher education* (pp. 206–230). Entebbe: Nkumba University.

— (2004). "Trials and joy of running a Ugandan university institution: Reflections of a peripatetic Vice Chancellor". Unpublished paper presented on March 30, 2004 at a workshop on a quality assurance framework for higher institutions of learning.

— (2005). Speech of Vice Chancellor on 8th Convocation of Nkumba University. Nkumba University Grounds, April 23, 2005. Entebbe, Uganda.

— (2006). "Uganda's aims of education: Mandate of schools and culture of foundation bodies". In *Nkumba University Education Journal*, 1, 1–14.

Settoon, R., Bennet, N., & Liden, R. (1996). "Social exchange in organisations: Perceived organisational support, leader-member exchange, and employee reciprocity". In *Journal of Applied Psychology*, 81(3): 219–227.

Shahanwaz, M. G., & Juyal, R., C. (2006). "Human resource management practices and organizational commitment in different organizations". In *Journal of the Indian Academy of Applied Psychology*, 32 (3): 171–178.

Sharbain, A., & Tan, K. (2012). "Pre-service teachers' level of competence and their attitudes towards the teaching profession". In *Asian Journal of Social Sciences and Humanities*, 1 (3): 14–22.

Shattock, M. (2004). "Re-balancing modern concepts of university governance". In *Higher Education Quarterly*, 56 (3): 235–244.

— (2004). "The Lambert Code: Can we define best practice?" In *Higher Education Quarterly*, 58 (4): 229–242.

Shawa, L.B. (2012). "The big-man syndrome as a security threat in Malawi: A critical theory perspective". In *Southern African Peace and Security Studies*, 1(2): 44–56.

— (2014). "The quest for a quality delivery of university education in Malawi". In *Mediterranean Journal of Social Sciences*, 5(17): 548–555.

Sheppard, A.L. (2013). "Learning styles and motives of postgraduate distance learners undertaking a United Kingdom professional doctorate". In *Journal of Perspectives in Applied Academic Practice*, 1 (1). [Online]. Retrieved on February 7, 2017 from http://jpaap.napier.ac.uk/index.php/JPAAP/article/view/40.

Shu'ara, J. (2010). "Higher Education Statistics: Nigeria Experience in Data Collection". Paper presented at the UNESCO Institute of Statistics Workshop on Education Statistics in Anglophone Countries, Windhoek 17-21 October 2010.

Sicherman, C. 2005. *Becoming an African university: Makerere, 1922–2000*. Trenton: Africa World Press.

Sifuna, D. (2012). "Leadership in Kenyan public universities and the challenges of autonomy and academic freedom: An overview of trends since independence". *Journal of Higher Education in Africa*, 10 (1): 121–137.

Ssekamwa, J.C. (1997). *History and Development of Education in Uganda*. Kampala: Fountain Publishers.

— (2008). *Prof. William Senteza Kajubi educating through quotable quotes: Birth of his legacy at Nkumba University*. Kampala: Nkumba University.

Ssempebwa, J., Bakkabulindi, F. E. K., & Sekabembe, B. (2012). "Ignoring Functionality as a Correlate of the Underutilization of Computer and Information Technology in Rwandan Higher Education Institutions". In *Makerere Journal of Higher Education*, 4(2): 293 – 310.

Ssempebwa, J., Eduan, W., & Mulumba, F.N. (2012). "Effectiveness of university bridging programs in preparing students for university education: A case from East Africa". In *Journal of Studies in International Education*, 16 (2): 140–156.

Ssesanga, K., & Garrett, R. M. (2005). "Job satisfaction of university academics: Perspectives from Uganda". In *Higher Education*, 50: 33–56.

Ssesanga, N.A.K. (2003). "Job satisfaction and dissatisfaction of university academics: Perspectives from Uganda". In *Uganda Journal of Education*, 4: 65-89.

Steele, C. (1997). "A threat in the air: How stereotypes shape intellectual identity and performance". In *American Psychologist*, 52 (6): 613–629.

Stewart, T. A. (1997). *Intellectual capital: the new wealth of organizations*. London: Crown Business.

Stroud, B. (2011). "The history of epistemology". In *Erkenntnis*, 75 (3): 495–503.

Stuart, L. H., Mills, A. M., & Remus, U. (2009). "School leaders, ICT competence and championing innovations". In *Computers & Education*, 53(3): 733 – 741.

Sum, W.W. (2005). "Safeguarding the quality of cross-border education: The role of governments and quality assurance bodies". Paper presented at the seminar on the theme, 'Establishment of cross-border education assessment mechanisms'. Held at Kunming, China, in May 2005.

Sveiby, K. E. (2001). "A knowledge-based theory of the firm to guide in strategy formulation". In *Journal of Intellectual Capital*, 2 (4): 344–358.

Swatos, W.H., Jr. (Ed) (nd.). *Encyclopaedia of religion and society*. [Online]. Retrieved on April 13, 2014 from http://hirr.hartsem.edu/ency/Motive.htm.

Tamale, G. D. (2007). "Reward management and employee job performance in institutions of higher learning using Uganda Christian University as a case study". Unpublished MEd. dissertation. Kampala: Makerere University.

TCU. (2010). *Students' guidebook for the central admission system for higher education institutions 2010/2011*. Dar es Salaam: Author.

Taylor, J., & Miroiu, A. (2002). *Papers in higher education: Regional university network on governance and management of higher education in South East Europe*. Bucharest: UNESCO.

TESSA (2011). [Online]. Retrieved on February 7, 2017 from http://www.tessafrica.net/images/stories/pdf/briefing_note_2_pager_v3.pdf. Accessed on 17/2/2011.

Teferra, D. (2011). "Graduate Un(der)employment and the Sparking of a Revolution in Africa". *International Network for Higher Education in Africa Editorial Series* [Online]. Retrieved on February 7, 2017 from https://www.bc.edu/research/cihe/inhea/editorial/archives/apr2011.html.

Teferra, D., & Altbach, P. G. (2003). *African Higher Education: An International Reference Handbook*. Indiana: Indiana University Press.

— (2004). "African higher education: Challenges for the 21st century". In *Higher Education*, 47(1): 21–50.

Teferra, D., & Knight, J. (Eds.). (2008). *Higher education in Africa: the international dimension*. Boston/Accra: African Books Collective.

The University of Malawi. (1998). *The University of Malawi Act (1974) incorporating the Amended Act of 1998*. Zomba: The University Office.

Tho, Q.T., Hui, S.C., Fong, A.C.M., & Tru Hoang, C. (2006). "Automatic fuzzy ontology generation for semantic web". In *IEEE Transactions on Knowledge and Data Engineering* 18 (6): 842–856.

Tiberondwa, A. K. (1998). *Missionary teachers as agents of colonialism: A study of their activities in Uganda 1877–1927*. Kampala: Fountain Publishers.

Tizikara, M. K. (1998). "Correlates of academic staff satisfaction in universities in Uganda". Unpublished Master's dissertation. Kampala: Makerere University.

Tjeldvoll, Welle-Strand and Bento (2005). "The Complex Relations between University, Society and State: The Ethiopian Predicament in Establishing a Service University". In *Journal of Higher Education in Africa*, 3(1): 51–75.

Tricker, R. I. (1984). *Corporate Governance*. Aldershot: Gower Publishing Company.

Trucano, M. (2005). *Knowledge Maps: ICTs in Education*. Washington, DC: infoDev & The World Bank.

Trusty, J. (2000). "High educational expectations and low achievement: Stability of educational goals across adolescence". In *Journal of Educational Research*, 93(6): 356–365.

Ugboro, I., & Obeng, K. (2001). *Managing the aftermaths of contracting in public transit organizations: Employee perception of job security, organizational commitment and trust*. Greensboro: School of Business and Economics.

UNESCO Institute of Statistics (2013). "Global flow of tertiary-level students". [Online]. Retrieved February 3, 2017, from http://www.uis.unesco.org/Education/Pages/international-student-flow-viz.aspx

UNESCO (1998). "Higher education in the twenty-first century: Vision and action". Final Report on the World Conference on Higher Education. Paris: UNESCO.

— (2002). "Forum on the impact of open courseware for higher education in developing countries: Final report" [Online]. Retrieved November 3, 2008, from www.wcet.info/resources/publications/unescofinalreport.pdf.

— (2005). *Cross-border providers of higher education.* Retrieved from http://www.unesco.org.

USAID/ FGN. (2009). *Basic education analysis report.* Abuja: Author.

Uvalic-Trumbic, S. (2008). "The UNESCO/OECD guidelines for quality provision in cross-border higher education". Paper presented at the seminar, 'Quality assurance in transnational education: From words to action'. Held at London, UK, in December 2008.

van der Stel, M., & Veenman, M.V.J. (2008). "Relation between intellectual ability and metacognitive skilfulness as predictors of learning performance of young students performing tasks in different domains". In *Learning and Individual Differences,* 18(1): 128–134.

van Dick, R. & Ullrich, J. (2013). "Identification and commitment". *In Management Journal,* 10: 349–354.

van Vught, F. (1994). "Autonomy and accountability in government/university relations". In J. Salmi & A. Verspoor (Eds.), *Revitalising higher education* (pp. 322–362). Oxford: Pergamon Press.

Vandenberghe, C., Bentein, K., & Stinglhamber, F. (2004). "Affective commitment to the organization, supervisor, and workgroup: Antecedents and outcomes". In *Journal of Vocational Behaviour,* 64: 47–71.

Veenman, M.V.J., & Verheij, J. (2001). "Technical students' metacognitive skills: Relating general vs. specific metacognitive skills to study". In *Learning and Individual Differences,* 13(3): 259–272.

Veenman, M.V.J., & Spaans, M.A. (2005). "Relation between intellectual and metacognitive skills: Age and task differences". In *Learning and Individual Differences,* 15 (2): 159–176.

Veličković, V. M., Višnjić, A., Jović, S. A., Radulović, O., Šargić, Č., Mihajlović, J., & Mladenović, J. (2014). "Organizational commitment and job satisfaction among nurses in Serbia: A factor analysis". In *Nursing Outlook*, 62(6): 415–427.

Venable, M. (2015). "What influences your career choice?" [Online]. Retrieved on February 4, 2017 from http://www.onlinecollege.org/2011/05/17/what-influences-your-careerchoice.

Vincent-Lancrin, S., & Pfotenhauer, S. (2012). "Guidelines for quality assurance in cross-border higher education: Where do we stand?" In OECD education working papers, No. 70. [Online]. Retrieved on February 4, 2017 from http://dx.doi.org/10.1787/5k9fd0kz0j6b-en.

Walter, W.P., & Snellman, K. (2004). "The knowledge economy". Annual Reviews [Online]. Retrieved on April 11, 2014 from http://www.stanford.edu/group/song/papers/powell_snellman.pdf.

Wayne, J.H., Casper, W. J., Matthews, R. A., & Allen, T. D. (2013). "Family-supportive organization perception and organizational commitment: The mediating role of work-family conflict an enrichment and partner attitudes". In *Journal of Applied Psychology*, 98(4): 606–622.

Wells, G. (2010). "Motive and motivation in learning to teach". [Online]. Retrieved on April 10, 2014 from http://people.ucsc.edu/~gwells/Files/Papers_Folder/documents/MOTIVEANDMOTIVATIONfinal.pdf.

Wenglinsky, H. (2002). "How schools matter: The link between teacher classroom practices and student academic performance". In *Education Policy Analysis Archives*, 10 (12):1–30.

Whitty, G., Power, S., & Halpin, D. (1998). *Devolution and choice in education: The school, the state and the market*. Buckingham: Open University Press.

Wikieducator (2011). "Towards an OER University: Free learning for all students worldwide". [Online]. Retrieved on April 11, 2017 from http://wikieducator.org/Towards_an_OER_university:_Free_learning_for_all_students_worldwide.

William and Flora Hewlett Foundation (2008). "Open Educational Resources (OER): Making high quality educational content and tools freely available on the web" — Retrieved November 13, 2008 from www.hewlett.org/Programs/Education/OER/.

Winzenried, A. (2011). "Information literacy landscapes: Information literacy in education, workplace and everyday contexts". In *Library Review*, 2 (60): 120–135.

Wokocha, A.M. (2005). "Education and deregulation in Nigeria: Presidential Address". In *Nigerian Journal of Educational Philosophy*, 12 (1): 1–7.

World Bank (2008). *African development indicators 2008/2009*. Washington, DC: World Bank.

Xiao, J. (2001). "Determinants of salary growth in Shenzhen, China: An analysis of formal education, on-the-job training, and adult education with a three-level model". [Online]. Retrieved on April 11, 2014 from http://www.tc.columbia.edu/centers/coce/pdf_files/d4.pdf.

Yukl, G. (2006). *Leadership in organizations* (6th ed.). New Jersey: Prentice-Hall.

Yusof, K. (2008). "University Governance in Malaysia". Paper presented at Regional Seminar on University Governance in Southeast Asian Countries, Luang Prabang, Lao PDR.

Zeleza, P.T. (2003). "Academic freedom in the neo-liberal order: Governments, globalisation, governance and gender". In *Journal of Higher Education in Africa*, 1(1): 149–194.

Zhao, F. (2003). "Enhancing the quality of online higher education through measurement". In *Quality Assurance in Education*, 11(4): 214–221.

Zimmerman, B. J. (2000). "Self-efficacy: an essential motive to learn". In *Contemporary Educational Psychology*, 25: 82–91.

Index

academic
 auditing 22
 bodies 27
 character 25
 development 116, 176
 freedom xxiii, 28, 60, 87, 199
 growth 116
 knowledge 73
 publishing 16
 staffing 25
 superpowers 22
accreditation agency (ies) 23, 60, 61, 62, 143
activity-based education 74
African Network of Scientific and Technological Institutions (ANSTI) 7
Association of Commonwealth Universities (ACU) 61
autonomous scholarship 94
basic research 94
branding campaigns 26
bridging programme 28
bureaucratic tendencies 111
career
 development 102, 145, 147, 151
 mobility 73
Catholic University of East Africa 23
Centre for Girls and Women's Education in Africa (CIEFFA) 54, 181
change management 35
civil society groups 3
classical political democracy 56
colonial universities 87
Commission for University Education (CUE) 23
communication
 innovations 2, 14
 skills 15, 79
community service 44, 60, 118, 141
competitive advantage 101, 102
computer literacy 15
consultancy culture xxiv, 88, 90, 91
course
 materials 28
 programme content 29
cross-border higher education (CBHE) 18, 19, 20, 21, 22, 25, 26, 27, 29, 30, 31, 32, 33
deregulated
 economy 57
deregulation
 of education 53
 policy 53
development
 needs 2, 71
 paradigm 3

developmental
  challenges 9
diffusive innovation 4, 14
digital communication 15
Diploma Entry Scheme 42
disciplinary
  literature 95
  specialisation 98
distance education 20, 153, 179, 192, 195
East Africa
  region 18, 19, 20, 22, 23, 25, 26, 30, 31, 32, 87, 139, 140, 180, 194, 197, 199
East African Community xiii, 19, 20, 31
economic
  development 5, 21, 127
  growth 3, 4, 57, 193
educated labour force 72
educational
  demands 19, 21
  philosophies 27
Education Policy Review Commission (EPRC) 38, 42, 44, 184
environmental resources 74
ergonomic comfort 62, 63, 66
Ethiopia xxix
external examination systems 22
extra-curricular seminars 88
faculty performance 103
fake degrees 22
fee-paying students (privatisation) 87, 140, 141
financial resources 25, 42, 113

foreign
  dependency 5
  education 29
gainful employment 77, 120, 151
gender sensitivity 60
General Agreement on Trade in Services (GATS) 21
general knowledge 73, 79, 83
Ghana xii, xxix, 2, 5, 7, 9, 10, 16, 17
global
  higher education market 70
  (ised) society 19
  knowledge 4
  North 25, 26
  South 25, 26
  technologies 5
health services 62, 63, 65, 67, 68
high education/ tertiary education 3, 4, 24, 50, 54, 181, 188, 197
higher education
  accreditation 30
  service delivery 60, 61, 62, 67, 68
human
  capital 21, 70, 71, 72, 74, 78, 82, 83, 101, 103, 134, 179
  resource development 5, 19, 49
ICT facilities/infrastructure 27, 142, 146
industrial age 1
information
  literacy 15, 16
  services 68

Institute of Teacher Education
    Kyambogo (ITEK) 37,
    41, 192
institutional
  governance 25, 60
  objectives 25
  partnerships 91
  peculiarities 24
  quality improvement 21
institution building xxiv, 86
institutions' performance 60, 62
intellectual
  abilities 75, 80
  capabilities 56
  capital xxiv, 99, 100, 101, 102,
    103, 104, 105, 106, 108,
    113, 116, 177, 179, 188,
    195
  culture 90
  developments 98
  disciplinary 93
  dispensation 93
  expansion 28
  life 88
  paradigm(s) 88
  potential 115
  property 72, 154, 159, 160
inter-disciplinary
  curriculum 87
  knowledge 98
international students 29, 58, 59,
    61–63, 65, 67, 68, 69, 178
interpersonal collaboration 111
intrinsic motives 77
ITEK xxi, 37, 41, 192
job
market 76, 119, 151
satisfaction 102, 145, 176, 177,
    181, 183, 185, 186, 187,
    203
Kajubi, Senteza William (Prof.)
    xxv, 34, 36–50, 197, 199
Kampala ix, xi, xii, xiv, xvi, xxvii,
    36, 63, 64, 85, 139, 177,
    178, 179, 185, 187, 188,
    190, 192, 193, 195, 199,
    201
Kampala International University
    (KIU) xi, xii, xiv, 63, 176,
    195
Kasozi, A.B.K (Prof.) ix, xxvi, 47
Kenya's Commission for Higher
    Education (CHE), 1985
    23, 28, 30
knowledge
  -based competencies 21, 74
  consumption 11
  dissemination 102, 154
  economy 4, 20, 118, 119, 125,
    131, 177, 195, 196, 203
  gap 59
  generation 3, 99
  production
    institutions 5
Kyambogo University xvi, 41,
    63, 64
labour
  economics 71
  market 60, 74, 118–126, 132,
    178
  performance 60

library services 62
lifelong learning 19, 20
local
  capacity 6
  needs 5
  science 2
long distance educational delivery 18
Makerere Institute of Social Research (MISR) ix, xvi, xxi, xxvi, 85, 90, 91, 94, 95, 96, 98
market-driven curriculum 87
matriculation examination 28
Mature Age Entry Scheme(s) 42
Mitchell, Philip Euen (Sir) iii, xxvii
multinational academic institutions 22
National
  development 2, 5, 6, 9, 14, 17, 49, 94, 118, 136
  granting councils 11
  science 2
National Council for Higher Education (NCHE) 2001 (Uganda) ix, 24, 30, 45, 47, 60, 62, 64, 67, 68, 143, 193
Nkumba University xii, xiv, 38, 45, 46, 47, 48, 64, 196, 198, 199
nomenclature 24
Nyerere Kambarage, Julius Mwalimu 31
organisation structure 102

partial knowledge 72
peer communication 4, 14
peer–to–peer communication 14
physical
  disabilities 54
  resources 140
policy-oriented centres 94
political
  constraints 59
  economy 96
post-colonial development 87
post-graduate education 88
post-graduation motives 70, 71, 76–78, 82, 83
poverty reduction 4
power point presentations 88
primary education 27, 40, 90
private universities 20, 23, 31, 45, 46, 47, 49, 50, 53, 66, 67, 68, 103, 106, 107, 108, 111–113, 115, 116, 117, 141, 142, 143, 150, 152, 197
professional
  bodies 60
programme mobility 18, 19
public
  enterprises 52
  intellectuals 94
  policies 51
  service programmes 76
  universities ix, 19, 23, 31, 43, 46, 47, 49, 50, 66, 67, 111–113, 116–120, 124, 132, 136, 137, 140, 141, 143, 150, 152, 188, 192, 199

utility 56, 57
quality
  assurance 20, 22–28, 30, 32, 58, 60–62, 130–132, 140, 143, 159, 160, 180, 181, 190, 194, 196, 200, 203
  information 61, 77
  relationship capital 102
research
  and development xxix, 8
  funding 93
Savannah Agricultural Research Institute (SARI) 9, 10, 13, 16
scholarly community 1, 96
scientific knowledge 72
secondary education 27, 28
social
  class 54
  competence 72
  development 8
  goods 54
  media 16, 17
  sciences 11, 12, 91, 92, 95, 97, 98
  stratification 54, 55
  transformation 57
societal economy 74
stakeholder communication 14
stock of knowledge 70, 71, 72, 83
strategic planning 25, 131
student
  enrolment 19
  mobility 18, 29, 32

Tanzania Commission for Universities (TCV) 2005 23
task-specific knowledge 73, 79, 83
teaching
  -intensive institutions 115
  methods x, 49, 123, 124
technical innovations 4
technology
  exchange 21
  transfer 3, 5, 6
Technology Achievement Index (TAI) 13
think tank 94
transfer of science 3
tuition fees 19, 54
Uganda 5, 9, 24, 27, 28, 30, 31, 34, 36–40, 42, 45, 47, 48, 49, 50, 59, 60, 64, 67, 68, 71, 83, 85, 86, 99, 101, 105–108, 110–115, 139, 140, 176, 184, 188, 190, 192, 193, 196, 197, 198, 199, 200, 201
  Christian University (UCU) 47, 64, 200
  Law Society 61
  Martyrs University (UMU) xi, xiv, 47, 64
universal access 53
Universities and Other Tertiary Institutions Act (2001) xxiii, 60
universities' recreation services 67

university
  budgets 28
  education 23, 34, 36, 38, 39, 42–45, 48, 49, 53, 54, 57, 76, 92, 113, 126, 129–133, 135, 137, 139, 140, 141, 195, 198, 199
  governance xxvi, 103, 127, 128, 130–133, 135, 136, 138, 185, 198
University College of London xxvii
visual literacy 15, 16

World Bank xiii, 7, 71, 83, 131, 140, 182, 183, 185, 188, 190, 196, 197, 201, 204
World Trade Organisation 21

www.ingramcontent.com/pod-product-compliance
Lightning Source LLC
Chambersburg PA
CBHW071408300426
44114CB00016B/2221